The Sterling Huck Letters

STERLING HUCK

...age Hill Press™

Nashville, Tennessee

A Division of Thomas Nelson, Inc.
www.ThomasNelson.com

Published by Rutledge Hill Press, a division of Thomas Nelson, Inc., P.O. Box 141000, Nashville, Tennessee 37214.

Photos of Sterling Huck by Mark DeLong.

Designed by Brecca Theele.

Library of Congress Cataloging-in-Publication Data

Huck, Sterling, 1962–
        The Sterling Huck letters / Sterling Huck.
            p. cm.
        ISBN 1-40160-035-2 (pbk.)
        1. Letters—Humor. 2. American wit and humor.   I. Title.

    PN6231.L44 H83 2002
    814'.6—dc21   2002073914

                        Printed in the United States of America

                        02 03 04 05 06 — 5 4 3 2 1

Contents

Preface

Dear Reader,

I wrote the first Sterling Huck letter on June 3, 1995. It was to the Space Center in Alamogordo, New Mexico. I'd read an article about Ham, the chimpanzee the U.S. sent into space back in the early '60s, and how his remains were now buried on the grounds of the place. Posing as an author researching a book on simian intelligence, I wrote to the Space Center, asking for information on Ham. I wondered if his brain had been preserved and where I might see it. I also delicately suggested that I might like to exhume the body of the "chimp-o-naut."

A week later I got a reply, a helpful letter from the Space Center with the phone number of the professor who trained Ham, along with a thick packet of documents - some of which I'm convinced were formerly top secret government memos. Remember, we were in a space race with the Russkies. There was even a handsome portrait of the smiling Ham in his space suit.

I should write more of these letters, I thought. And so I did. Hundreds of them. Now, seven years later, here are some of my favorites in a book. There are even photos and sketches to add to the fun.

I hope that you enjoy it.

Best Regards,

Sterling Huck

Sterling Huck
May 2002

P.S. - Some names have been changed or omitted to protect the overly sensitive. For the handful of companies who refused to let me reprint their responses, I've provided a brief summary of the contents of their letters.

A c k n o w l e d g m e n t s

Thanks to Larry Stone, Bryan Curtis, Jennifer Greenstein, Amy Powers, Christy O'Flaherty, Tracey Menges, Brecca Theele, and all my friends at Rutledge Hill Press, my parents (is this what you sent me to college for?), Jimmy and Nettie, Molly Felder (always my first and best audience), Mickey Grimm, Brad "Jerry DePoot" Jones, Robin Eaton, Richard "Buddy Hackett" Julian, Lydia Hutchinson, Ashley Cleveland, Kenny Greenburg, Garry Velletri & Diane Painter, Pat Sansone, Jenifer Jackson, Amy Rigby, Mike Grimes, Tony Miracle, Kip Kubin, Jill Sobule, Heather Johnson, Joe Pisapia, Marc Pisapia, James Hagerty, Ross Rice, Bill & Laura Lloyd, Griffin Norman, Frank Goodman, Gordon Richard, Allison Inman, Jim Pitt, Leonard M. Bankman, Phil Nel, Patrick Dobson, *FHM Magazine*, my friends at Copy Solutions, Beth Speltz, Greg Gianforcaro (the real Indigo Matahi), Mark DeLong and Trey Mitchell for the great photos, Kristof & Elisabeth for the German translation, Ham the space chimp, Don Novello, James and Stuart Wade and Ted L. Nancy for blazing the letter trail, Peter Sellers, Woody Allen, Albert Brooks, Dudley Moore and Peter Cook, *SCTV*, Martin Short, David Sedaris, Ben Stiller, Bob Odenkirk, David Cross, Jon Stewart and Conan O'Brien for continued inspiration.

A special thank you to Cliff Goldmacher for making my letters required reading in his studio, and an extra special thank you to Tia Sillers for putting my letters in the right hands.

A very extra special thank you to Laura Hudgins and Laura Beth Durham, whose charm and persistence on the phone made all the difference.

And finally, to all the companies, organizations and individuals who were good sports, I thank you.

Sterling Huck
May 2002

P.S. - Oh, and thanks to you for buying my book!

"I have this
problem . . ."

August 27, 1998

Banana Patch Nudist Resort
P.O. Box 1107
Kealakekua, HI 96750

Dear Friends,

I know that at Banana Patch you are accepting of "alternative lifestyles." It's a place where your guests can get back to the "bare necessities" of life and feel free of social restrictions. With that in mind, I'm hoping that you'll be accepting of me, a vacationer who needs a special place to go.

My necessities are more "bear" than "bare." I am a man who likes to dress up in a bear suit. This passion began years ago when I worked in a traveling carnival. I won't bore you with my history, but suffice it to say, there aren't many places I can go in my bear suit without being ridiculed or chased or shot at or arrested (I've experienced all).

Wearing the bear suit around my apartment is not satisfying. I need to be outdoors where I can run and leap and splash and frolic in streams.

I'm hoping that you'll extend an invitation to me to vacation at Banana Patch the third week of September. Your guests could be made aware that I'm not an actual bear, but a friendly guy in a bear suit (I'll be nude underneath). I have several different suits - Kodiak, Polar, Brown, Panda - if you'd prefer one or the other. And of course I'll respect your guests' privacy as I hope they will respect mine.

Thank you for your kind understanding. I look forward to hearing from you.

Sincerely,

Sterling Huck
3901 Whitland Ave. #27
Nashville, TN 37205

www.bananabanana.com

The Banana Patch
PO Box 1107
Kealakekua, Hi. 96750

Aloha Sterling,
Thank you for your interest in my accommodations.
I don't have a problem with you wearing a bear suit or anything else for that matter.
My cottages are separate and private and my guests have plenty of private space.
So what you wear is up to you.
As far as running, leaping, and splashing, you do have your oun hot tub but I would rather
you stay out of the fish ponds.
My one bedroom cottage, with full kitchen, king bed is available the third week of Sept.
It is $85.00 per night plus tax.
I ask for a deposit of half your stay,- Personal check to me Reggie Mitchell
What nights would like to reserve.
I look forward to hearing from you.
Aloha,
Reggie

P.S. - If you really have a need to frolic in the fish pond I would
need to charge you more,- To cover any damage to plants etc.
I only have one openning the 3rd week of Sept.
So if you want to reserve it you should call as soon
as possible 1-800-988-2246

Aloha
Reggie

March 31, 1998

Bekins
330 S. Mannheim Rd.
Hillside, IL 60162

Dear Bekins,

This June, I'll be moving from Nashville, TN to Reno, NV. I'm looking for a moving company that will not only handle my personal belongings (including a vast collection of scrimshaw) with care, but accommodate a special request.

For the past few years, my wife's grandmother has been living with us. While Grandma Ruth can be sweet when she wants to, lately she tends to be obstinate and a bit sullen. It has to do with the move. Though I've assured her she's coming with us, Grandma Ruth insists that she will remain in her favorite chair, a large blue recliner, no matter what happens. Indeed, she hasn't left the chair in two weeks.

My question: would it be possible for Bekins to move the large blue reclining chair with my Grandma Ruth in it? I believe she would be happier if she could remain in the chair during the van ride from Nashville to Reno. This continuity would ensure a smooth transition between the old and new home for her.

I realize that moving van trailers are usually packed to the ceiling with a family's belongings, but maybe we could clear a comfortable space for my grandmother. I've heard that Bekins is alone in the field of moving companies when it comes to special requests such as this. Thank you for your help. I look forward to hearing from you.

Sincerely,

Sterling Huck
3901 Whitland Ave. #27
Nashville, TN 37205

BEKINS

April 22, 1998

Sterling Huck
3901 Whitland Ave. #27
Nashville, TN 37205

RE: Potential Move

Dear Mr. Huck:

Bekins Van Lines Company
Move Management Services
330 South Mannheim Road
Hillside, IL 60162-1852
(708) 547-2000

Patricia A. Faragia
Director

Please forgive the delay in responding to your correspondence regarding a special request for a potential move to Nevada.

The delayed response was due to the fact that we engaged our experts at Bekins Van Lines to come up with a way to handle your request. I regret to inform you that after many discussions we are unable to find a viable, safe and legal solution that would allow us to move Grandma Ruth in her large blue recliner.

However, we would like to assure you and Grandma Ruth that we will, if given the opportunity, move her blue recliner and all belongings with the utmost care and handling. Further we will place Grandma Ruth's favorite chair in the location of her choice in your new home.

We thank you for the opportunity to respond and regret that Grandma Ruth and chair can not travel together in the van.

Please let us know if we can be of any service to you in the future.

Sincerely,

Patricia A. Faragia

April 7, 2002

Pietro Verdi Underwear
Strada Santa Barbara 5
61043 Cagli PU
Italy

Dear Pietro Verdi,

I have a slightly unusual problem and I'm turning to you, as leaders in the underwear industry, in hopes that you can accommodate me.

If you're familiar with the history of human evolution, you'll know that most people are born with what is called a "vestigial tail." This indentation, located near the base of the spine, is a ghost of an appendage that once hung from our bodies in bygone eras. It's a reminder that we're not so different from our reptilian and amphibious cousins!

Unfortunately, in my case, the tail is not vestigial. It is very real, about 26" long and tapered like a fleshy exclamation point. I'm now 32 and despite some harrowing, insult-laden years in school, I'm what I consider a fully-adjusted normal man, with a good job, a lovely wife and two beautiful children (neither have tails).

Though it's always been difficult finding clothing that will both accommodate and hide my tail comfortably, the most problematic article in my wardrobe has been my underpants. Sometimes I've worn them backwards to allow my tail an aperture through which it can dangle freely (though the placement is not quite right). This of course leaves me with a solid cotton sheath on the front side, which is inconvenient and uncomfortable. Other times, using a scissors, I've cut a crude hole in the back of otherwise good shorts, only to have them fray and tear after a few wearings.

The solution would seem to be underpants with dual openings, front and back, and I have every confidence that you can design them for me. Please let me know how I can order a few dozen of these special underpants with the extra aperture for my tail. If you'd like me to come into your headquarters for a fitting, perhaps I could arrange it. Thanks for your understanding and help. I truly appreciate it.

Warm Regards,

Sterling Huck
3901 Whitland Ave. #27
Nashville, TN 37205
USA

29 April 2002

Dear Sterling,

Wouldn't plastic surgery have been easier in the long run . . . or do you, secretly, feel too attached to your tail . . .

Best Wishes,

Peter Greene
Pietro Verdi & C.

November 25, 1997

United Nations
United Nations Plaza
New York, NY 10017

Dear Gentlemen,

I'm writing you with a request. I'd like to know how I could get one of
those special headsets you have at the U.N. that automatically
translates a foreign language into English. You see, I'm a big fan of
French movies but I don't speak the language. And because my eyesight
is not so good, I have trouble reading the subtitles. I think if I could just
plug in some of your United Nations headphones to my television set,
then I could enjoy these movies more. Also, if you have a headset that
translates Hindustani, it would help me, because my landlord, Mr.
Parbhubhai Patel does not speak very good English and we sometimes
have disagreements related to the upkeep of my apartment.

Please let me know the price of the U.N. headphones (the French set is
more important to me) and how I can order a pair as soon as possible.

Thank you.

Regards,

Sterling Huck
3901 Whitland Ave. #27
Nashville, TN 37205

UNITED NATIONS NATIONS UNIES

POSTAL ADDRESS—ADRESSE POSTALE UNITED NATIONS, N.Y. 100··
CABLE ADDRESS—ADRESSE TELEGRAPHIQUE UNATIONS NEWYORK

REFERENCE

Dear Sir/Madam,

Thank you for your recent letter.

We appreciate your interest in the United Nations but, unfortunately, we are unable to assist you for the following reason(s):

_____ The requested publication has not yet been printed. Kindly inquire at a later date.

_____ The publication is not issued by the United Nations. You may wish to consult your local library.

✓ The United Nations has no information on your topic.

_____ The requested material is out of print. Enclosed is other information which might be useful.

_____ Material on your topic is no longer available. You may wish to consult your local library or a United Nations depository library as indicated on the attached list.

_____ Material not available from this office. Please write directly to the specialized agency or related international organizations indicated on the attached list.

_____ This Office maintains no mailing list.

_____ The item(s) requested is/are sales items and may be ordered prepaid, from:

     United Nations Publications
     Room DC2-0853
     New York, N.Y. 10017
     Tel. 1-800-253-9646 E-Mail: Publications@un.org

We regret that we cannot be more helpful.

                Sincerely yours,

                Hasan Ferdous, Chief
                Public Inquiries Unit
          Department of Public Information

April 17, 2002

Chiva Som Spa & Resort
87 Sukhumvit 63
Bangkok 10110
Thailand

Dear Chiva Som,

I am interested in staying at your beautiful resort for five days beginning June 17, 2002, but before I make my reservations I want to find out more information.

I am a semi-professional ventriloquist and I always travel with my partner, Little Sir Pitney. Since he hates to be left alone, I'd like to feel free to bring him around with me as I enjoy the many features of Chiva Som. Are there any house rules about having a ventriloquist assistant (he doesn't like the word "dummy") at the pool or the restaurant? Little Sir Pitney is usually well-behaved, although sometimes when he hears a loud, startling noise, he jumps and makes a shrieking sound that is reminiscent of the sound Shemp Howard of the Three Stooges used to make when he got scared. He (Little Sir Pitney) doesn't speak unless spoken to, but I'm sure that many of your guests will be so delighted to make his acquaintance that they'll want to talk to him.

On the subject of meals: in the past, other hotels have been happy to provide a special "high chair" for Little Sir Pitney, so I'm guessing that won't be a problem. I think you're really going to be fond of the little guy. When he stayed at Harrah's, he was voted "Favorite Guest Of The Month" and given a shiny paper crown to wear. He's also very excited about the spa, because he loves the sauna. Dry heat has a kind of soothing, therapeutic effect on his wooden body. When I told him about your sauna, he asked, "Is it coed?" He can be such a randy little fellow sometimes!

If we could settle these few trivial matters before I book a room, it would be wonderful.

Please let me know about your services for Little Sir Pitney. The two of us are looking forward to being your guests at Chiva Som!

Yours Sincerely,

Sterling Huck
3901 Whitland Ave. #27
Nashville, TN 37205

27 April 2002

Sterling Huck
3901 Whitland Ave. #27
Nashville, TN 37205

My dear Mr. Sterling,

I am delighted to have heard from you, and will be delighted also to make the aquaintance of your assistant, little Sir Pitney.

He has been referred to me as I am the Health and Wellness director, and it seems as though he may need a lot of the treatments we have available here!!!

Firstly, if he is so short, he must have had a hormone problem since birth, and whilst we dont presume to cure diseases, we do have plenty of nurses at hand to check his blood levels etc. Mind you, the nurses are all very attractive, and I want to ensure that he is on his best behaviour with them at all times OK?

Body composition analysis should reveal some very interesting statistics, from which we can put him and you on a tailor-made programme of activities. I also reccomend for him a full body oil massage, this will make him feel more supple and be good for his 'skin'. I dont reccomend water treatments for him though, but I definitely think you should try them to relax you !! We also have a 'metamorphosis' treatment, and that may well bring out some very interesting changes in him....please do have a look at our website for more information www.chivasom.com.

He sounds like quite a handful, and I would suggest plenty of morning meditations and yoga to calm his mind and spirit.

When he has done that for a few days, he will feel like a new man, and you will see the sparkle return to his eyes.

A wonderful healthy diet of spa cuisine will put his digestive system back on track, and his energy levels will increase no end. He may no longer need so much support from you, and you should find him more energetic and effective in his role as your assistant.

11th Floor, Modern Town Building
87 Sukhumvit 63, Bangkok 10110,
Thailand.
Tel : +66(0) 2711 6905-10
Fax : +66(0) 2381 5852

You said that in some other resorts he was given special treatment, but here in Chiva Som, we give ALL our guests special treatment, you and he will be indulged and pampered back to full health, and he will need no special crowns as he will develop a healthy glow which you will never have seen before!!

Now then; you say he loves the sauna - good -but he MUST wear proper attire. If he is naughty, I personally will ensure that he is put on the 'detox diet', and he wont be allowed to partcicpate in any of our fun activities (I will diagnose his naughty behaviour as an imbalance, a cry for help, and treat it accordingly!!).

Also, you say that if there are any loud noises he shreiks a lot - well, this sounds to me like he has a nervous disorder, and I highly reccomend the de-stress treatments - maybe you and he are working too hard, and so Chiva Som sounds like just the 'time out' you both need !!

Of course we will be able to accomodate his special needs, and yours too, and I look forward to welcoming you both on the 17th June.

warm regards
Sarah Noble
Corporate Director, Health & Wellness, Chiva Som

Little Sir Pitney, where would you like to go for our vacation?

Chiva Som!

September 19, 1996

Amateur Athlethic Union of the U.S.
3400 W. 86th St.
P.O. Box 68207
Indianapolis, IN 46268

Dear Sirs,
    As I'm certain you have access to a vast network of sports league information, I'm hoping you can help me. I'm the coach of a donkey basketball team here in Nashville. We're called the "Whoop-Yer-Asses." The problem is, there's a lack of opposing teams for us, so mostly we're inactive. As it's rather expensive to care for and feed seven burros, we're hoping to connect with other donkey basketball teams around the Southeast and Midwest regions, so we can maintain our franchise. Perhaps we could form a league, with your assistance.
    Any information you could provide would be greatly appreciated!

                    Regards,

                    Sterling Huck

                    Sterling Huck
                    3901 Whitland Ave. #27
                    Nashville, TN 37205

STERLING,
    OUR NETWORK DOESN'T
INCLUDE DONKEY BASKETBALL —

            SORRY   HK

February 11, 1998   NO REPLY

AT & T
32 Ave. of the Americas
New York, NY 10013

Dear Alpha, Tango & Tango,

If you're confused by that salutation, it will only confirm my suspicion that
your company has permanently shunned some of your oldest customers, like
myself. Namely, the customers who still rely on the second "T" in your
company name - the telegraph.

I got my first telegraph in 1918 - I was 9 years old - and have always believed
it to be the superior form of communication. In fact, to this day, I don't use a
telephone. Never have, never will. Over the years, I've built up a network of
friends and diplomatic contacts around the country and the world, and we've
corresponded, sometimes sending important secret messages, other times just
"small tapping" over the wire. But lately, that correspondence has faltered.
Signals are breaking up. Transmissions are failing. The blame, my friends,
must be laid at your multi-national corporate doorstep. I've seen your TV
commercials. I know what you're doing. It's all about telephones and this e-
mail business.

Will you rob an 88-year old man of his pleasure and fun (Foxtrot-Uniform-
November) by denying him his dots and dashes?

Best Regards,

Sterling Huck
3901 Whitland Ave. #27
Nashville, TN 37205

June 16, 1998

Serta Mattress Co.
325 Spring Lake Dr.
Itasca, IL 60143

Hello Perfect Sleepers,

I'm organizing a 25th anniversary gathering for Vietnam Veterans here in Nashville. It will be held the weekend of August 21st at the Scottish Inn. I'm trying to give the vets the best entertainment possible. So far, I have tentative commitments from the popular 70s rock band Redbone ("Come And Get Your Love") and comedian/ventriloquist Willie Tyler & Lester. As a headliner, I'd like to book the sexiest lady in show biz, Joey Heatherton.

I know that Ms. Heatherton has long been closely associated with Serta "Perfect Sleeper" mattresses, so I'm hoping that you can help me realize this dream. It's not only for me, but for the Vietnam Vets and for America!

When I mentioned the name Joey Heatherton, some of the vets got misty-eyed, then began to reminisce in an animated manner about a USO show back in the early 1970s that featured Joey, clad in a camouflage negligee, writhing around on a Serta mattress, cooing a slow version of "Dream A Little Dream Of Me," with special lyrics about the Vietnam War.

Would you please contact Joey Heatherton and let her know about this very special gathering of the veterans. I'm sure she'll be interested. Or, if you'd prefer, you can put me in touch with her booking agent and we can talk price.

I thank you Serta, as do America's fighting men. We can't wait to see Joey!

Best Regards,

Sterling Huck
3901 Whitland Ave. #27
Nashville, TN 37205

P.S. - Indigo Matahi, the general manager of the Scottish Inn, asked if there was any way he might be able to get Serta to donate some new mattresses to the hotel if Joey Heatherton does the performance.

WE MAKE THE WORLD'S BEST MATTRESS

Friday, June 19, 1998

Sterling Huck
3901 Whitland Avenue #27
Nashville, TN 37205

Dear Mr. Huck:

I have received your letter of June 16 regarding the 25th anniversary gathering for the Vietnam Veterans. In response to your question of getting in contact with Joey Heatherton, I must inform you that Serta has had no affiliation with Ms. Heatherton since the early 70's. However, we know that she appeared in the Playboy Magazine April-97 issue, you may try contacting Playboy Magazine to get in touch with Ms. Heatherton's booking agent.

We are a major supplier of Hotels throughout the U.S. if Indigo Matahi is interested in purchasing our mattresses please have him contact Fred Gibson the Vice President of Contract Sales at (800) 426-0371.

Sincerely yours,

Celest Winfrey
Manager of Consumer Relations
Serta, Inc.

July 3, 1995

Parker Brothers
P.O. Box 1012
Beverly, MA 01915

Dear Parker Brothers,

While recently attending a large Greek wedding in Lancaster, PA, I met an elderly gentleman who bore an uncanny resemblance to the little "Monopoly Guy" who appears on your Chance and Community Chest cards.

This man had the same compact physique, walrus mustache, bright eyes and - when he removed his silk top hat - clean domed head.

I couldn't get over the likeness. When I mentioned it to the elderly gentleman, he made an expression that I recognized from the "Bank Error In Your Favor" community chest card. It was an odd moment. I found out later that my little friend couldn't speak a word of English. I also found out - and this is why I am writing - that his name was Nick Monopolous!!

Coincidence? Or have I stumbled onto the living model for one of America's favorite board game icons? What gives, Parker Brothers?

I look forward to hearing from you soon.

Yours Sincerely,

Sterling Huck
3901 Whitland Ave. #27
Nashville, TN 37205

Parker Brothers
P.O. Box 1012
Beverly, Massachusetts 01915-1894
Phone (508) 927-7600

July 17, 1995

Mr. Sterling Huck
3901 Whitland Ave. #27
Nashville, TN 37205

Dear Mr. Huck:

A Greek speaking MONOPOLY man....how interesting!!

We do not have any record of how "Rich Uncle Pennybags" happened to appear on our game in 1936, a year after we first published it. Perhaps it was Nick Monopolous...whose to question??

We sincerely appreciate your taking the time to write and wish you many hours of fun with Parker Brothers' games and toys.

Sincerely,

Consumer Relations Department

Consumer Relations

August 2, 1996

Charlton Heston
2859 Coldwater Canyon
Beverly Hills, CA 90210

Hello Mr. Heston!

I am organizing a convention on the subject of simian intelligence, called *Monkeyshines '97*, to be held in Mufreesboro, TN at the Scottish Inn the weekend of March 7-9, 1997.

Currently, I'm recruiting guest speakers. So far, I've secured Professor Robert Content, who in 1961 trained Ham, the famous "chimponaut" that "manned" one of NASA's first space capsules. I also have a tentative commitment from Stan Burns and Michael Marmer, the creative team behind *Lancelot Link, Secret Chimp*. And we may have a video montage tribute to Clyde, the orangutan from *Any Which Way You Can*.

Mr. Heston, we would be most honored to have you participate in the convention. As a <u>featured guest speaker</u>, you could share a wealth of information about your experiences making the classic *Planet Of The Apes*. I'm sure it would be enlightening, humorous and absolutely riveting for all those attending *Monkeyshines '97*.

I appreciate your consideration of this offer. Please let me know your fee for these kinds of engagements. Also, would you know how to get in touch with Maurice Evans, the actor who portrayed your nemesis, Dr. Zaius? Wouldn't it be wild if we could have the both of you facing off in point-counterpoint style just like you did in the Simian court of justice!

Thanks again. As one of your biggest fans (I even thought you were great in *El Cid*), I look forward to having you join us at the convention.

Kind Regards,

Sterling Huck
3901 Whitland Ave. #27
Nashville, TN 37205

KEPPLER
ASSOCIATES
INC.

December 17, 1996

Mr. Sterling Huck
3901 Whitland Ave. #27
Nashville, TN 37205

Dear Mr. Huck:

As the agent here that handles Tennessee I wanted to respond to your inquiry regarding Mr. Heston and Monkeyshines '97.

Mr. Heston does do public speaking one to two times a year in the spring and fall within a set tour. Unfortunately, he is unable to make any commitments for 1997 for several more months for personal reasons.

I appreciate your interest. Should you wish to discuss the matter with me further please call me at (703) 516-4000. I would also be happy to explore alternative ideas with you as we represent hundreds of personalities, journalists and businesspeople.

Sincerely,

Stephen U. Brush
Account Executive, Corporate Division

SUB
Enc.

August 17, 1996

Maxell Corporation
2208 State Rte. 208
Fair Lawn, NJ 07410

Dear Gentlemen,

I recently purchased some of your 90-minute "blank" tapes, and I put the word "blank" in quotation marks because I've discovered they were anything but that. I'd intended to make a birthday tape for my mother, with comedian Myron Cohen on one side and the songs of Robert James Waller on the other, but I forgot to hit the record button on my tape deck. On playback I discovered my error. Then I heard the voices. Faint as they were, I distinctly heard a conversation between two men. One had what sounded like a pronounced lisp, as he said the phrase "fortuitous situation" several times. It's a difficult phrase for someone with that speech affliction. This talking went on throughout Side A of your "blank" tape, fading in and out. The gist of the conversation seemed to be the one man (with the lisp) trying to get the other to invest in a piece of exercise equipment called "The Ab-dicator." It's all very odd, I think.

I'm hoping you can shed some light on the situation. Are you selling recycled tapes?

Best Regards,

Sterling Huck

Sterling Huck
3901 Whitland Ave. #27
Nashville, TN 37205

maxell
MAXELL CORPORATION OF AMERICA

1400 PARKER ROAD, CONYERS, GEORGIA 30207, (770)922-1000, FAX: (770)483-5893

August 28, 1996

Sterling Huck
3901 Whitland Avenue #27
Nashville, TN 37205

Dear Mr. Huck:

I apologize for this situation and would like to thank you for your patience and giving us the opportunity to respond to you. We want you to be completely satisfied with your Maxell purchase. If you should ever find any of our products to be unsatisfactory, please let us know.

By keeping us informed, you help us to maintain our high quality standards. Information gathered from our customers is forwarded to our manufacturing facilities for use in our continuing improvement programs. It is the efforts of our concerned customers that help us to make our products the best they can be.

Please send these tapes to my attention, Darlene Partain Only, for an evaluation. I will forward our findings to you. We do not sell used or recycled tapes and the tape should have been unused and have no recording. Please include the location of purchase with the return.

Thank you for contacting us and for your continued support of Maxell products.

Sincerely,

MAXELL CORPORATION OF AMERICA

Darlene Partain
Consumer Relations Department

Enc: 108900 - 2 XLII 90

September 10, 1999

Starbucks
P.O. Box 3717
Seattle, WA 98124-3717

Dear Starbucks,

I was glad to see that your nationwide expansion has finally led you into Nashville, Tennessee. Having downed Starbucks lattes and grande mochas in many other cities, I was one of the first in line at your flagship coffee house here in my own hometown.

I wanted so much to be a "regular," but only a month after Starbucks opened here, I was told by the manager, a Mr. Bobby Huffine, that I was never to step foot on the premises again. The confusion (and anger, on Mr. Huffine's part) has apparently been caused by me playing a few tunes on my pennywhistle in Starbucks.

I've been playing pennywhistle all my life, so I'm no amateur. I have a vast repertoire of Irish favorites, a few of which I played in Starbucks (to the delight of the other patrons), including "Galway Bay," "The Isle Of Innisfree," "O' Shaugnessy Owes Me Money," "Hey Boyo (Get This Thorn Out Of Me Foot)," and "That Tumbledown Shack In Athlone."

Mr. Huffine said that my pennywhistle playing was "distrupting [sic] the atmosphere" and asked me to stop. But I can't turn down a request and there were two sweet moppets who asked me for one more tune. I was halfway through "When Irish Eyes Are Smilin'" when I was unceremoniously ousted from Starbucks and given a threat that if I returned they would "notify the authorities."

In my defense, if I might say, my pennywhistle playing is the kind of thing that could give character to your establishment, separating it from the identical Starbucks around the country. People would say, "Oh, that's the place where that little guy with the sparse red beard practices pennywhistle every afternoon. C'mon, let's go there!"

Since the incident, I'm all broken up inside (I've even composed a sad, yearning melody on my pennywhistle, which I call "Goodbye Starbucks"). I'd like to be able to return to the Starbucks in Nashville. Could you please talk to Mr. Huffine and tell him I'm sorry. I'll leave my pennywhistle outside next time. I can't live without Starbucks!

Regards,

Sterling Huck
3901 Whitland Ave. #27
Nashville, TN 37205

Starbucks Coffee Company
Customer Relations
PO Box 3717
Seattle, WA 98124-3717

Sterling Huck
3901 Whitland Ave #7
Nashville, TN 37205

37205-1340 10

After polling their local employees,
Starbucks could find no trace of either a
Bobby Huffine or a man with a sparse
red beard playing the pennywhistle.

File it under "Grande Mystery."

April 24, 2002

Orion Shipping
Orion House,
Deans Road,
Swinton, Manchester,
M27 0JF UK

Dear Orion,

I am a granite sculptor, currently working on the Mount Rushmore Extension Project. Perhaps you read about it in a recent National Geographic article. We're adding two more presidential heads to the great monument for the upcoming 65th anniversary celebration.

One of the casts for the mammoth stone heads, modeled after our ninth president, Martin Van Buren, is being sculpted by a crew near Montevideo, Uruguay. When it is finished this August, we would like to transport it, via one of your ships, to Seattle, Washington, where it will then be taken to South Dakota for the final mounting.

The giant Martin Van Buren head cast is approximately 52 cubic feet and weighs 1,100 lbs. (it's hollow). As part of the curing process requires that the Uruguayan granite be exposed to sunlight, I would ask that the head of President Van Buren be openly displayed on deck of your ship during the sea journey. It's interesting to note that Van Buren was a seafaring man in his youth (nicknamed Cappy), so maybe we can take that connection as a good sign!

Please let me know if you can transport the giant stone head of former president, Martin Van Buren, and also an estimate of the price. Together we'll be part of American history.

Kind Regards,

Sterling Huck

Sterling Huck
3901 Whitland Ave. #27
Nashville, TN 37205

ORION
SHIPPING & FORWARDING LIMITED

BIFA
Freight Service Award
1998

Orion House, 78 Deans Road,
Swinton, Manchester M27 0JF
Tel: 0161-794 7356.
Fax: 0161-794 7364.
www.orionshipping.co.uk

BS EN ISO 9002
Certificate No. FS 11842

1st May 2002

Sterling Huck
3901 Whitland Ave. #27
Nashville
TN37205

Dear Sir

RE: Mount Rushmore Extension Project

Thank you for your interest in Orion Shipping but I am afraid we can not help you with your project as we do not like dealing with big heads.

"1100 lbs (it's hollow)" come on......

Don't now how you make your money from this con but thanks for giving us a laugh.

Yours sincerely

DAVID REAVEY
Managing Director

February 20, 2002

Ben & Jerry's Ice Cream
30 Community Drive
South Burlington, VT 05403-6828

Dear Ben & Jerry,

My name is Sterling Huck. Every night for the past two weeks, I've dreamt of new ice cream flavors. No sooner does my head hit the pillow than I'm hurtling past the Haagen-Daas nebula, beyond the 31 Flavors of Baskin-Robbins, to find myself face to face with huge colorful tubs of ice cream I've never before encountered.

Unfortunately, I never get to taste these wonderful new ice cream flavors in my dreams. But the names float into my subconcious via a low seductive male voice. Think of Darth Vader in a smoking jacket. That's the voice.

If you like any of these dream flavors, feel free to invent the recipe and market them:

Wolfgang Amaretto Mocha
Baking Soda Peroxide Whitening Chocolate
Ethan Frome's Wintry Trudge Fudge
James Coco's Cocoa Waistline Miracle
Adolph Green's Denture Friendly Fudge
Vanilla Scrod Swirl
Dutchmasters Cookies n' Stogies
Thrilla In Vanilla
Colonel Constantinople's Big Blast O' Chocolate
Einstein's E = Mocha Squared

Maybe you could call these flavors Ben & Jerry & Sterling's Ice Cream. What do you think?

I love your ice cream!

Best Regards,

Sterling Huck
3901 Whitland Ave. #27
Nashville, TN 37205

Sterling Huck
3901 Whitland Avenue
#27
Nashville, TN 37205

Dear Sterling:

Thank you for sharing your creativity with us! Some of our best-selling flavors were suggested by consumers just like you, including Cherry Garcia., Chubby Hubby. and Chunky Monkey.! Before we're able to consider your idea and share it with others at Ben & Jerry's, we need you to agree to a few terms; otherwise, it will just sit in our files here in the Consumer Affairs department. Please pardon our formality. Our legal department says that in all fairness, we must let everyone know what our acceptance policy is all about. We can't do anything these days without the lawyers getting involved!

Enclosed is the "Ben & Jerry's Agreement and Policy Concerning Suggestions". Please read through it and if you accept and agree to everything that is written, sign the last page and send it back to us using the enclosed postage-paid return envelope. If you're under the age of 18, please review the policy with your parents or guardian and have them sign it with you. If we don't receive your signed agreement within a reasonable length of time, we'll assume you don't want us to consider your idea and in our files it will stay, never to be shared with others. Such a shame!

If you have access to the internet, you can send us your idea using the "Suggestion Box" in the Consumer Assistance section of our website. We're at www.benjerry.com. Check us out!

Thanks for caring and taking the time to write us. If you have any questions, please give us a call at (802) 846-1500 between 9:00a.m. and 5:00p.m. EST Monday through Friday. Ask for Consumer Affairs. If we decide to use your idea, you'll be hearing from us!

Flavorably Yours,

Consumer Affairs

Enc.

30 Community Drive • South Burlington, Vermont • 05403-6828 • Tel: 802/846-1500 • www.benjerry.com

April 9, 1996

Halls Brothers
Whitefield Ltd.
Dumers Lane
Radcliffe, Manchester
N26 England

Dear Gentlemen,

I recently attended a fabulous brunch at the home of Dr. Indigo Matahi and his wife, here in Tennessee. On a table the size of a small tennis court there was a spread of delectable foodstuffs - eggs benedict, potato pancakes, fried okra, miniature sausage medallions and a lot more. But I was most taken by one unusual offering, muffins with a strong hint of eucalyptus and menthol in the center. When I inquired about them, the hostess told me that the recipe came from the Halls Clear Sinus Cookbook that she'd ordered by mail from your company.

Can you please tell me how I get my copy of the Halls cookbook? Mrs. Matahi said there was also a delicious recipe for "Vap-O-Action Chicken."

Regards,

Sterling Huck
3901 Whitland Ave. #27
Nashville, TN 37205

CONSUMER AFFAIRS DEPARTMENT

Adams/American Chicle/Parke-Davis/Shaving Products/Warner Wellcome Consumer Healthcare

201 Tabor Road
Morris Plains, NJ 07950

Phone: (800) 223-0182

April 25, 1996

Mr. Sterling Huck
3901 Whitland Ave. #27
Nashville, TN 37205

Dear Mr. Huck:

Letters from our valued consumers are always welcome and whenever possible, we try to be of assistance.

We have read with interest your letter addressed to our affiliate in England and, after checking many different sources, we are unable to come up with a Halls cookbook. This is the first time anyone here has heard of it!

We are truly sorry we can not be of any assistance to you in this matter. However, we are enclosing a Halls coupon for your use. Thank you for taking the time to write and for your interest in Halls Cough Drops.

Cordially yours,

CONSUMER PRODUCTS GROUP

Mary Richardson

Mary Richardson, Director
Consumer Affairs Department

MR/wl

7896270

May 29, 2001

Crowne Plaza
1601 Biscayne Blvd.
Miami, FL 33132

Dear Crowne,

I will be attending the 3-day Sanyo convention at your hotel this August. I've heard that you're tops in accommodating guests, so I'm writing ahead with a special request.

Because of a severe bronchial condition, I must sleep outdoors. With your permission, I would like to pitch a tent on the hotel grounds. If there are two trees in close proximity, I would also like to set up a hammock. This way, I can wake up in the morning, have some sterno-warmed coffee and go straight to the seminars and motivational talks. I understand that you won't be able to offer the usual amenities - cable TV, mini-bar, continental breakfast, free ice - but I'll still feel like I'm part of the convention and the Crowne family. If you'd like, I could pay a small "squatter's fee."

Thanks for your understanding. Please send me a map of the grounds with your suggestions (make an "X") where I can set up camp.

As part of my lung therapy, I inhale and exhale into a chromatic harmonica.

Kindest Regards,

Sterling Huck
3901 Whitland Ave. #27
Nashville, TN 37205

WYNDHAM MIAMI
BISCAYNE BAY

June 5, 2001

Sterling Huck
3901 Whitland Avenue # 27
Nashville, TN 37205

Dear Mr. Huck:

I am in receipt of your letter dated May 29, 2001 and thank you for your interest in our hotel.

We have researched our convention calendar and have no planned conference for Sanyo in August. Nevertheless, this property is in a high rise city property with no trees or grassy area suitable to pitch a tent.

If you would like information on local campground facilities, please let us know and our concierge will forward you the information.

Again, thank you for your interest in our hotel.

Sincerely,

Duane Rohrbaugh
General Manager

March 5, 1998

American Express
3 World Financial Center
200 Vesey St.
Lobby Level
New York, NY 10285

Dear Gentlemen,

As a man who has recently come into a lot of money, I'm now shopping around for the ideal credit card. While interest rates and credit limits are certainly important to me, what's more crucial is the actual size of the card itself. Most plastic cards, as you know, are a standard size of approximately 3 1/2" x 2", but this will not do.

I carry a special wallet that was given to me by my financial benefactor, T. Ambrose Forsythe, a self-made multi-millionaire. The inner pouches and photo holders of this wallet are smaller than those in the average man's billfold. This wallet has brought me happiness and extreme wealth, so I'm reluctant to change to another wallet. Given my status as a Fortune 500 climber, other financial institutions have been happy to accomodate me with "slim-line" cards.

I need a special American Express credit card measuring 2" x 1 3/8". Otherwise, the design can be identical with the handsome green background, the roman warrior guy and my name in raised type: Sterling Huck.

Please let me know how quickly you can deliver my slim-line American Express card. I have a lot of money ready for you.

Regards,

Sterling Huck
3901 Whitland Ave. #27
Nashville, TN 37205

American Express bent over backwards to accommodate Sterling, but couldn't alter the world standard size for credit cards.

They did mail him a nice faux leather card holder, which he keeps in his top desk drawer next to his X-Ray Specs and Silly Putty.

February 23, 1998

Zenith Electronics Corp.
1000 Milwaukee Ave.
Glenview, IL 60025

Dear Zenith,

I recently bought one of your 27" Zenith brand TV sets. While the clarity of the sound and picture is wonderful, I am experiencing a strange problem.

The TV set gives off a strong odor that smells like pizza. More specifically, a pepperoni and green pepper pizza. At first I thought maybe I was imagining this or that I was catching a whiff of what my downstairs neighbor was cooking (I live in an apartment complex and can usually tell what he's making, be it Steak-Um's or some sort of Mexican dish). But soon I discovered that the pizza smell was coming from the TV. I put my nose right up to it. Pizza. Very strong. There's no smoke or anything, and really the smell is rather appetizing. But I think that maybe in another week or two, I won't feel so happy about the pizza smell.

I called a TV repairman but he laughed and said something about "dibodes" and "caploads" needing to be broken in. Unfortunately I can't return the set because I bought it off the back of a truck from a guy wearing a big turquoise cowboy hat. So I'm turning to you because I've heard that Zenith is tops in customer service and they believe in the personal touch.

Should I open the back of the TV and look inside? There's that warning that says "Danger! Electric Shock!" but that's only if its still plugged in while I'm tinkering with it, right? Is it possible that one of your assembly line workers at Zenith was eating a slice of pizza (pepperoni and green pepper) and maybe dropped part of it inside this particular set? Maybe everytime I turn on the set, the pizza scrap is being reheated and that's where the smell is coming from.

In the meantime, I'll watch my old TV. It's a Zenith too. I've had it for 20 years and never a problem.

Regards,

Sterling Huck
3901 Whitland Ave. #27
Nashville, TN 37205

ZENITH ELECTRONICS CORPORATION 1000 MILWAUKEE AVENUE GLENVIEW, ILLINOIS 60025-2493 (847) 391-8752

March 15, 1998

Mr. Sterling Huck
3901 Whitland Ave.# 27
Nashville, TN 37205

Dear Mr. Huck:

Thank you for your letter regarding your Zenith television.

Regretfully, we are unable to advise you about the problem you are experiencing without visually inspecting your set. For service assistance, we suggest you contact one of the authorized Zenith servicers:

Electronic Service Center
3711 Nolensville Road
Nashville, TN 37211
615-331-4629

HI-Tech Service of TN
2934 Nolensville Road
Nashville, TN 37211
612-331-9250

We appreciate you bringing the matter to our attention. If you need further assistance, please call (847) 391-8752.

Very truly yours,

Zenith Response Center

File#175786

July 5, 2002

Alexis Hotel
1007 First Avenue
Seattle, Washington 98104

Dear Alexis,

I'm interested in staying at your hotel from August 28-31. This will be my first time in your great city, and I'm looking forward to seeing the sights. I've heard that you are very accommodating of your guests, so I thought I'd write ahead to let you know of a potentially uncomfortable situation.

I look exactly like Lex Luthor. You may remember, he is Superman's arch-nemesis, a warped scientific genius with a shiny bald head. A wily fiend with designs on conquering the world. Though my appearance is identical to Lex Luthor's, my personality is most certainly not. I am not power mad or megalomaniacal or seething with ambition and malevolent schemes. I am laid-back. I run a small crafts shop in Nashville, TN called "Beads N' Things." And while I admit to having my misanthropic moments like anyone else, I'm not an inveterate hater of mankind, nor do I wish to ultimately enslave the people of earth.

More differences: Lex Luthor lost his hair in an accidental laboratory explosion. I lost mine to male pattern baldness. He blames Superman for the accident. I don't blame anybody. It's just genetics. I haven't patented any diabolical inventions such as an earthquake maker or atomic death ray, nor do I know how to synthesize kryptonite into "Luthorite." I don't live in a glass-enclosed city of strange geometric proportions, a massive fortress-like citadel, a gigantic man-made meteor, a lead-lined subterranean lair, or a hidden laboratory masquerading as a chemical manufacturing plant on the outskirts of Metropolis. I live in a two-bedroom apartment with bad water pressure. I don't use aliases or false identities such as Carlyle Allerton, Professor Clyde or The Defender. My name is Sterling Durwood Huck. I'm not married to Ardora, nor do I have a sister named Lena Thorul, who has ESP. I am single, with no siblings. I'm not inspired by the lives of Ghengis Khan, Attila The Hun, Blackbeard or Al Capone. I look up to Abe Lincoln and Mother Teresa. And let's be honest, Lex Luthor is insane. The closest to insanity I've ever come is once when I agreed to ride on the Texas Thunder roller coaster with a friend.

I'm sorry to have to go to such great lengths to differentiate myself from Lex Luthor, but when you see me walk into your hotel lobby, you will understand. You may even have a reflexive reaction that causes you to blurt out, "That guy looks just like Lex Luthor!" You see, aside from the clean-plated dome head and icy blue eyes, I am very tall, well-proportioned and I enjoy wearing shimmery tunics of silver and gold. It's a fashion choice, that's all. It has no deeper meaning or insidious planet-threatening connotations.

I would appreciate it very much if you could have your hotel staff and guests refrain from staring at me, saying "Aren't you Lex Luthor?" or asking if I'll pose for a photograph. It has been a problem for me in the past, and I grow weary of these tiresome pleas from the masses. One day they will know the truth.

Thank you for accommodating my needs. I look forward to hearing from you.

Sincerely,

Sterling Huck
3901 Whitland Ave. #27
Nashville, TN 37205

A WORK OF ART

Mr. Sterling Huck
3901 Whitland Ave. #27
Nashville, TN 37205

July 10, 2002

Dear Mr. Huck,

Thank you for your letter dated July 5.

We would be very pleased to welcome you to the Alexis Hotel during the specified dates of August 28-31 of this year. We have availability in all room types at this time and encourage you to call us at (206) 624.4844 or toll-free at (888) 850.1155 to make reservations. Our room rates vary from $225 to $295 and rates for our suites range from $305 to $455 during that time. We will be glad to describe the many amenities of each room type to you.

Regarding your request for discretion on the part of our staff and guests, we assure you that the Alexis Hotel has welcomed many actors, singers, statesmen, stateswomen and other notable dignitaries in the past with great success. Your situation is unique and certainly deserving of special consideration. Most of our celebrity guests are the actual person that they look like. Therefore, they know that they will be asked for photographs, signatures and in the case of former Attorney General, Janet Reno, the odd baby-kissing opportunity.

Our Director of Loss Prevention, who ironically somewhat resembles The Riddler, one of Batman's rivals, handles our covert VIP entrances and exits. He has devised a relatively foolproof manner in which to access the hotel in a discrete and private fashion. His suggestion will ensure that you will not be disturbed by our other guests, should they recognize you from your movie roles in Superman I through Superman IV (my personal favorite). The plan involves using a separate entrance in the rear of the hotel, which will allow you to enter in relative comfort. In order to protect your anonymity, we can offer you the use of a linen cart, with clean linens of course, that you may ride through the corridors to reach your room. If another guest is using the hallway at the same time as you, you can hide under these linens until the guest passes. Please be assured that our guests' comfort and safety are our priorities. That is why we use the highest grade fabric conditioner which only enhances the comfort of our 300 thread-count linens. Depending on staffing levels, we can offer a laundry attendant to drive you from the secret entrance to your room or suite.

If you elect to dine in the restaurant, our concierge could arrange a hat or wig for your use during your stay. However, the Alexis Hotel offers 24-hour room service featuring many items from our famed restaurant menu.

Thank you again for your letter and the heads-up on your situation. We look forward to welcoming you to Seattle. The temperatures in August can reach the upper 80's, in case you have a short-sleeved version of your shimmery tunics.

Best regards from your friends at the Alexis Hotel,

Marco Baumann
Front Office Manager

1007 FIRST AVENUE
AT MADISON
SEATTLE WASHINGTON 98104
TEL.206.624.4844
FAX.206.621.9009

February 2, 1997

McDonald's
McDonald's Plaza
Oak Brook, IL 60521
Customer Relations Dept.

Dear Gentlemen,

On a recent visit to Scotland, I was delighted to find some
of the first links in your worldwide restaurant chain. What a
welcome sight, to see your familiar golden arches reaching up
to the sky above the wee town of Kirkintillochogue. On my
first visit, just as I was about to plonk down a few quid for
a Big Mac, the pretty lass taking my order suggested I try
the famous "McHaggis Sandwich." Boy, I'm glad I did! What a
treat - the succulent tender calf's liver minced with suet,
onions and your special seasonings. Needless to say, I
returned every afternoon of my three-week visit for the
"McHaggis Sandwich."

My question is, when can we expect to see this tasty sandwich
on the McDonald's menu here in the good old U.S.A.? I hope
soon, because I've been boasting to everyone I know, whipping
up some anticipation for the McHaggis in my little corner of
the world.

Regards,

Sterling McHuck
3901 Whitland Ave. #27
Nashville, TN 37205

McDonald's did not deny the
existence of the McHaggis Sandwich,
saying that tastes vary and every country
is entitled to their own twist on
the Big Mac formula.

Does that mean there's
McWienerschnitzel?

April 25, 2002

Treecycle Paper
PO Box 5086
Bozeman MT 59717

Dear Treecycle,

I've heard that you are leaders in the paper industry, so maybe you can help me out with a problem.

I am allergic to over fifty different fabrics, including cotton, rayon, polyester, wool, nylon, satin and silk. If my skin comes into contact with any of these I break out in bright red hives, then shake uncontrollably. As you can imagine, this has made the simple act of dressing almost impossible for me. For the past few years, I've worn mostly plastic shawls and ponchos, but now I fear that I'm developing an allergy to them as well.

About the only material that I am able to withstand is paper. Envelopes, notebooks, cereal boxes, toilet tissue, magazines - none of these things bother me. What I'd like to do is have a wardrobe designed for me entirely out of paper.

Of course, I realize that these outfits would be, by their nature, disposable, so I'd be interested in ordering large quantities. I'm not finicky about style - how could I be? - but I do like the look of belted jackets like the kind Truman Capote used to wear. Also, very loose fitting trousers. I won't need paper underpants. Here are my sizes: 36w 28l (trousers), 18 1/2, 34-35 (shirts), 38R (jacket) and 11 (shoes). White paper is fine, but maybe some various colors would be nice too.

If you'd like I could come in for a fitting, or put you in touch with my tailor Mr. Bermudez. Thank you for helping me live a full, productive life.

Kindest Regards,

Sterling Huck
3901 Whitland Ave. #27
Nashville, TN 37205

TREECYCLE
P.O. Box 5086 · Bozeman, Montana 59717

May 1, 2002

Sterling Huck
3901 Whitland Ave. #27
Nashville, TN 37205

Howdy Sterling,

This is not the sort of thing we do. We sell paper, we do not make paper or paper products. I do not even know where you would start. Maybe with a hospital and ask where the paper gowns come from. Good luck.

Rick at Treecycle

July 3, 1995

Clowns of America International
P.O. Box 570
Lake Jackson, TX 77566

Dear Sirs,

I'm writing to you because I'm afraid of clowns. Not just a little afraid, but terrified. Ever since I was a boy, I've been tormented by recurring nightmares about this one clown in particular - he's a midget in a white satin suit and pointy hat, like the outfit Caruso wore when he played Pagliacci (though Caruso wasn't a midget). The dwarf clown in my dreams has a hideous laugh and wields a small obsidian dagger, which thank god, he's never used on me, though I can tell you (with years of cold sweat on my back), he's come close. I'm now in my thirties and still I have these nightmares.

I've only confessed this phobia to a few people, but no one seems to sympathize much or have any answers. Since you are obviously a kind of information clearinghouse for clowns and clowning, I wondered if you could recommend any books that might help, or any "fear of clowns" support groups.

Thank you very much for your help. I await your reply with hope of relief.

Sincerely,

Sterling Huck
3901 Whitland Ave. #27
Nashville, TN 37205

P.O. Box 570
Lake Jackson, TX 77566
July 15, 1995

Dear Sterling:

I've read your letter many times in hopes of finding the correct way to answer your questions and fears. First, my heart goes out to you! Clowns are supposed to invoke laughter and joy, not fear. Knowing many of the clowns in the U.S. and in several other countries I can attest they are a good hearted bunch. They, like me, would be distressed to hear of your plight. We are just ordinary people in unusual clothes and make-up that like to make people laugh .

My idea to help is this: If you knew more about us you would see that knife welding is not in our nature. I don't know if it will help, but I have given you a free subscription to our magazine. You can read about us and what we are about. I am also including a copy of the Clown Prayer and our Code Of Ethics. Maybe the more knowledge you have of clowns the easier it will be to eliminate your nightmares.

As I wrote this letter I realized that I too have had a recurring nightmare. Mine was concerning tornadoes. The town I lived in had two (1948 and 1955). Then when the wind would blow or thunder would roll I would want to hide my head, even if it was under a newspaper. Believe me I understand your fear. Later I became a pilot and as part of my training I studied the weather and learned how tornadoes were formed, what part of the cloud spawned them and their life cycle, and how to recognize the beginnings of one. As I came to understand, my fear seemed to go away. Maybe yours will too.

Yours in clowning,

David "Shorty" Barnett
Business Manager
Clowns of America International

January 8, 1996

NO REPLY

Campbell Soup Company
Camden, NJ 08103-1701

Dear Gentlemen,

I'm writing to register a complaint. In recent weeks, I have received multiple phone calls from a recorded voice that says, "Soup's On!" then proceeds to list different varieties of soup that your company offers.

The first time I got one of these calls I thought perhaps it was the prelude to some promotional campaign or contest, so I remained on the line. After the recorded voice - which seems to belong to a man of Jamaican descent - listed the soups, he then tallied off ingredients, nutritional information and directions on how to prepare the soup. It was as if he was reading from the side of a soup can. It seemed like it might go on indefinitely. I hung up right in the middle of Cream Of Celery.

But the calls have continued, and now number up to 8-10 per week. Some come at rather inappropriate hours. Last night, I was awakened out of a sound sleep at 2:13 am by the phone. The voice on the other end said, "Soup's On!" And I heard the faint sound of steel drum music behind him.

If possible, I wish to be removed from the list for this promotional soup campaign, if indeed you are behind it.

Thank you for your attention to this matter.

Regards,

Sterling Huck
3901 Whitland Ave. #27
Nashville, TN 37205

March 11, 2002

NO REPLY

Odor-Eaters
1101 Westchester Ave.
White Plains, NY 10604
Attn: Customer Service

Dear Odor-Eaters,

For many years, I was a seafaring man, spending months at a time on boats, schooners and ships. In 1978, I contracted gangrene in my left leg. At the time, I was in the middle of the Black Sea, far from any medical facilities. The first mate of the ship, a good man named Matahi, amputated my leg at the knee and replaced it with a sturdy wooden peg. At first, I only intended to keep the peg temporarily, until I could be fitted for a more modern prosthetic replacement. But time went by and I grew fond of the peg. It became part of my seafaring persona, if you will, and lent me a Stuyvesant-esque grandeur. I am now 68 years old and happy to be retired from my days upon the ocean. Mostly I stay home and whittle.

I am writing with an unusual request, but I trust that you will have the solution. My aging peg-leg is beginning to rot, and because of that, it sometimes gives off a kind of sulfury odor. As a man who inhaled many a foul smell at sea - fish guts, oil spills, various carcasses, etc. - I can handle the odor. But it's hard on my loved ones. My dear sister constantly complains about the smell from my peg leg. Actually, it was her suggestion that I contact you. Is it possible you could devise a kind of peg-leg Odor-Eater? Maybe a spongy wrap-around tourniquet that would absorb the smell and help preserve what's left of my wooden leg. The width of my peg-leg is approximately 4 1/8".

I appreciate your understanding in this situation and look forward to hearing from you soon.

Best Regards,

Sterling Huck
3901 Whitland Ave. #27
Nashville, TN 37205

March 17, 1998

Chancellor Helmut Kohl
Marbacher Strasse II
D-6700, Ludwigshafen Rhein
Germany

Hello Chancellor,

As an important politician and man of the people, I know you have many admirers not only in Germany, but around the world. I believe I have your number one admirer living under my roof. It's my son Kevin. Though he's only eleven, he has a keen interest in world politics and is constantly reading history books, political biographies and the daily newspapers. I'm almost ashamed to admit it, but Kevin knows a lot more about the political scene than his dear old dad.

Of all the presidents, kings, prime ministers and leaders, Kevin has singled you out as the one he'd like to emulate. He calls you "the only true politician of the '90s." He keeps a Helmut Kohl scrapbook and has several pictures of you, framed and hung on his bedroom wall, along with some Atlanta Braves pennants and a poster of the rock group Blues Traveler. When I ask Kevin what it is about you that he admires so much, he says, "The Chancellor cares about people. He's not a selfish, corrupt politician. Our own president could take some lessons from him."

Well, sir, Kevin has a birthday rapidly approaching - on June 5th, he'll be 12 - and my wife and I are planning a surprise party. Of course, we realize you're an extremely busy man and that Germany is a long way from Tennessee, but we'd like to extend an invitation to you to attend Kevin's 12th birthday party. He would be absolutely beside himself with excitement if you showed up. Kevin is taking a beginning German class in school, so maybe even the two of you could converse a little (perhaps you could pretend you were a fruit vendor and have Kevin ask you about the price of your apples).

If you can't make it to the party, I understand, but perhaps you could send a videotaped greeting or some kind of card to Kevin Huck. The boy's crazy about you, Mr. Chancellor.

Thank you for your kind consideration. Keep up the good work.

Kind Regards,

Sterling Huck
3901 Whitland Ave. #27
Nashville, TN 37205

BUNDESKANZLERAMT

Bonn, zum 5. Juni 1998
Telefon 02 28 / 56 - 2085
oder   02 28 / 56 0

An
Kevin Huck
3901 Whitland Ave. # 27

Nashville, TN 37205
USA

Lieber Kevin,

der Bundeskanzler hat von Deinem Vater erfahren, daß Du am 5. Juni 1998
Deinen zwölften Geburtstag haben wirst.

Der Bundeskanzler gratuliert Dir dazu sehr herzlich und hofft, das Du auf der von
Deinem Vater für Dich vorbereiteten "Überraschungsparty" viel Spaß mit Deinen
Freunden haben wirst. Weil Dein Vater in seinem Brief dem Bundeskanzler u.a.
auch über Dein großes Interesse an der internationalen Politik berichtet hat,
übersendet er Dir als Andenken an Deinen Ehrentag das Buch "Facts about
Germany und ein Foto, das der Bundeskanzler für Dich mit seiner Unterschrift
versehen hat. Sicher kannst Du in dieser Broschüre noch viele interessante Dinge
über Deutschland finden, die Du noch nicht kennst.

Für die Zukunft wünscht Dir der Bundeskanzler alles Gute, insbesondere Glück,
Gesundheit und viel Erfolg in der Schule.

Mit freundlichen Grüßen

Gabriele Korb-Wiegand

Dear Kevin,

The Chancellor learned from your father that y ou will have your birthday on June 5th, 1998.

The Chancellor sends you his sincere congratulations and hopes that you will have lots of fun with your friends on the "surprise party" prepared by your father. Since your father told the Chancellor in his letter, among others, of your great interest in international politics, he sends you as remembrance of your day of honor the book "Facts About Germany" and a picture, which the Chancellor signed for you. Certainly you will find many interesting things about Germany which you may not know yet.

For the future, the Chancellor wishes you all the best, especially luck, good health and much success in school.

With Best Regards,

Gabriele Korb-Wiegand

Roll Over, Thomas Edison . . .

September 15, 1998

Porsche Cars
100 West Liberty St.
Reno, NV 89501

Dear Porsche,

I was thrilled to read in the latest issue of *Stickshift Magazine* about your special 1999 XK-1 Model equipped with the cloaking device. The article didn't supply much information, but said it would be possible, with the touch of a button, to render the entire vehicle invisible, in the same way the Klingons do with their ship on Star Trek.

Some questions: How long can the car stay invisible? Is it just for a few seconds or for minutes at a time? Does it use extra gas? The reason I ask is because there's this guy named Cappy who lives on my street. Every time I drive by his house, he waves me down, walks over to my car, then talks about this operation he's going to have on his leg.

I've dreamt about a cloaking device that would enable me to drive undetected, right past Cappy's house. And now you've made one!

Another question I had, will the cloaking device make me invisible too? It might look funny to see me moving along at 30 mph in a seated position with no visible means of propulsion! Of course it wouldn't stop my neighbor Cappy from waving me down though. He'd still be telling me about that friggin' leg operation.

Would you please send me information about the new Porsches with the cloaking device? Thank you so much.

Best Regards,

Sterling Huck
3901 Whitland Ave. #27
Nashville, TN 37205

PORSCHE

October 28, 1998

Porsche Cars North America, Inc.
980 Hammond Drive
Suite 1000
Atlanta, Georgia 30328
(770) 290-3500 Fax: (770) 290-3700

Mr. Sterling Huck
3901 Whitland Ave.
Nashville, TN 37205

Dear Mr. Huck:

Thank you for taking the time to write to us. Porsche Cars North America, Inc. appreciates your interest in the Porsche product.

However, at this time we do not have a device such as the one mentioned in your letter, nor do we anticipate having one in the near future. We would nevertheless, love to have a copy of this article if you still have it.

Once again, thank you for your interest.

Sincerely,

Melody Lyons
Customer Commitment Assistant

April 26, 2002

Wheaton Moving Company
8010 Castleton Road
Indianapolis IN 46250-0800

Dear Wheaton,

I need to enlist the services of the best movers in the business, and on a tip from a trucker friend of mine, I'm contacting you. He said, "Wheaton will do right by ya."

I am an archeologist of some renown. If you read the *National Geographic*, you may remember me as the fellow who captured the leviathan near the Gulf of Kutch near Jamnagar, India. Recently, while digging at a site near Tagish Lake in the Yukon Territory, I unearthed a yeti. This magnificent, rare creature is encased in a block of solid ice, approximately 10' x 8' x 4'. I can only estimate the weight, but I'd guess about 1,100 lbs.

With your expert assistance, I want to move the frozen yeti from Tagish Lake to my research facility in Nashville, Tennessee. It's crucial that the yeti be preserved exactly as found. This means that your movers will not only have to exercise extreme care in handling the ice block, but they will have to make sure that it DOES NOT melt.

Perhaps you could pump in liquid nitrogen or dry ice to maintain a Yukon-like atmosphere in the trailer of your truck. You're the experts, so I'll leave these details up to you.

If the yeti should thaw out, I couldn't guarantee the safety of your drivers. The virile creature stands nearly 8-feet tall, is covered in thick gray fur and has razor sharp teeth and claws that can easily rip through metal. It would only take a few swipes of its claws for it to escape.

The yeti is basically gentle, but should he feel disoriented or trapped, which he surely would if he woke up in the back of your truck, he would go berserk.

Thank you for your understanding of this delicate situation. I need to move the yeti as soon as possible.

I look forward to hearing from you.

Best Regards,

Sterling Huck
3901 Whitland Ave. #27
Nashville, TN 37205

WORLD WIDE MOVING

29 April 2002

Mr. Sterling Huck
3901 Whitland Ave. #27
Nashville TN 37205

Dear Mr. Huck:

Your letter of 26 April has been forwarded to my attention, and congratulations on your most amazing discovery. The fact that you unearthed Sasquatch is not amazing in itself, as that was only a matter of time; the fact that you discovered him near Tagish Lake boggles the mind, as all odds were that it would be found somewhere east of Port Radium. This information has been verified by a staff member who has personally conversed with Yeti, hence his personal knowledge of locale. Unfortunately, my staff member will be crushed to learn of the demise of his friend but it will solve the mystery of why the letters suddenly stopped.

Regarding your request for logistic assistance, we certainly are the company who can achieve the impossible. Having reviewed you estimated specs, we have three problems which must first be overcome before we can progress into any form of pricing or scheduling:

1. The encasement of 10'x 8' x 4' is an actual volume displacement of 320 cubic feet. Under normal conditions, the ice layer would convert into roughly 64 pounds per cubic foot, thereby producing a tare weight of 20,800 pounds. Add to this the weight of the average mature male Yeti, and we are dealing with some 21,600 pounds. Specialized rigging equipment would have to be positioned, and the closest availability of such equipment would be on the Baldwin Peninsula;

2. The 10' measurement presents a problem, as enclosed vans have standard door apertures of just under 8'. As you so carefully outlined, only enclosed an enclosed van with extreme climate control can be used for transport, requiring the use of a highly specialized piece of equipment known as a "Van Stretcher". This item extends the metal skin of the trailer to an acceptable size, and upon release of tension, forms a metal skin around the contents. Refrigeration at zero to >30 degrees (Fahrenheit) is recommended, and liquid nitrogen propellants can be equipped within the trailer;

3. While we do own one such piece of specialized equipment, it is unfortunately unavailable. Currently through mid 2004, the stretch van is on the Loch Ness Monster World Tour, and then on reserve for the Osmond Family with Marilyn Manson "Free Tibet" tour.

I wish that we could be of greater assistance to you, and wish you (and Yeti) all the best of luck.

Budd Cardone, Vice President
Wheaton World Wide Moving

July 25, 1996

Omega Institute
260 Lake Drive
Rhinebeck, NY 12572
Programming Dept: New course idea

Dear Omega,

I'm writing to present a course idea that I think would be perfectly suited to the new age curriculum of your institute. What follows is a brief description:

The Empowered Grocery Shopper - How many times have you been faced with the myriad choices in a local supermarket, only to feel paralyzed and impotent staring at twenty brands of paper towels? I will show you how to reverse the power dynamic of the situation and put you in control of your shopping.

A few of the many topics discussed include - Barcodes: Friend or Foe?; Right-brained guided selection vs. left-brained unconscious humanization of food; Creating boundaries between you and other shoppers; The reality shift of frozen food aisles; 21 new ways to look at circus peanuts; Check-out line meditations of peace and patience.

As both a former assistant manager of Orange Julius and high school English teacher, I feel I am uniquely qualified to teach this course. If you're interested, we could develop it together for your next semester. I look forward to your reply.

Sincerely,

Sterling Huck
3901 Whitland Ave. #27
Nashville, TN 37205

150 Lake Drive, Rhinebeck, NY 12572   *phone* 914-266-4444   *fax* 914-266-4828   *website* www.eomega.org

August 14, 1996

Sterling Huck
3901 Whitland Ave. #27
Nashville, TN 37205

Dear Sterling -

Sorry it took so long to respond to your very important course proposal to
Omega. As a co-founder + catalog director, I have never been as intrigued
and powerfully moved. I'm still pondering the barcode mystery. Please send
more! I'm sure you have other course descriptions within. If you need help,
request my "Unlocking The Course Description Within" tape for just
$ 12.99.

Love,

Elizabeth Lesser

October 30, 2001

Imperial Products
70 High St.
Newcastle-Upon-Tyne
DH9 7SK England

Dear Imperial,

For years, I've been drinking everything from milkshakes to Milk of Magnesia through your fine imported straws. I like the regular ones, but I love the crazy straws.

As a part-time inventor, I'm always dabbling in my laboratory. Recently, after accidentally running an Imperial straw through a Bunsen Burner, I came up with an idea that I believe could revolutionize the world of straws, and be extremely lucrative for us both. I call it the "Certifiably Insane Straw."

It takes the crazy straw concept one step further. I'm envisioning five varieties:

Manic Depressive Straw - This straw will surprise you with its unpredictable moods. One minute, it will extend itself coquettishly out of a drink towards your mouth. The next it will shrink, disappearing beneath the surface of your beverage, letting out sad, intermittent bubbles of distress.

Schizophrenic Straw - Five straws, all different lengths and widths, linked to one single stem. Even its colors change. One minute, a flirty yellow-red striped design, the next a dark Calvinist gray. Which straw will draw out your beverage today? (Also available in a 7-straw size)

Psychopathic Straw - Keep your eye on this one! It can jump out of your glass, hide in dark corners, then wrap its tough plastic tubing around your neck. If this straw was an actor, it would be Robert Mitchum in *Cape Fear.*

Passive Aggressive Straw - Designed with a double uptake valve, this straw delivers a little "extra kicker" with every sip. Watch your eye. It's the straw that says "Gotcha!"

Catatonic Straw - Your powers of suction will be no match for this motionless straw, which can sit in a glass of the most effervescent ginger ale imaginable and feel absolutely nothing.

Let us work together to bring "Certifiably Insane Straws" to the world! I look forward to hashing out the details with you soon.

Kind Regards,

Sterling Huck
3901 Whitland Ave. #27
Nashville, TN 37205
USA

Imperial

Imperial Products
70 High St.
Newcastle-Upon-Tyne
DH9 7SK England

8 November 2001

Sterling Huck
3901 Whitland Ave.
#27
Nashville, TN 37205
USA

Dear Sterling,

Thank you for your letter. It made for very entertaining reading. Those of us who read it feel that it may be you, not your straws, that are certifiably insane.

We wish you all the best of luck with your future inventions.

Sincerely Yours,

Clive Hopkins
Consumer Dept., Imperial Products

April 16, 2002

Braintree District Council
Causeway House
Bocking End, Braintree
Essex CM7 9HB England

Dear Braintree,

I would like to visit your town this summer as a street vendor. The product I'm selling is called "The Hourglasses." Combining stylish eyewear and the finest in timetelling, it's a bold and convenient accessory. The handsome eyeglass frames are equipped with two tiny hourglasses, one for hours (on the right), one for minutes (on the left). And the hourglass sand comes in five colors, including pink.

I've included a rough sketch of The Hourglasses for your inspection. Please let me know if you think the good people of Braintree would enjoy "The Hourglasses."

Kindest Regards,

Sterling Huck

Sterling Huck
3901 Whitland Ave. #27
Nashville, TN 37205
USA

P.S. - I also sell His 'n' Hers Birdbaths.

HOURS!   MINUTES!

"THE HOURGLASSES"
by Sterling Huck

Our ref:	ST/mkts
Your ref:	
Ask for:	
Direct Dial No.:	Mr. S. Taylor
Ext:	2317
Date:	3rd May 2002

BRAINTREE

DISTRICT
COUNCIL

email: simta@braintree.gov.uk

Community & Leisure Services
Causeway House Braintree
Essex CM7 9HB

Tel: 01376 552525
Minicom: 01376 557766
Fax: 01376 557726
DX 56210 Braintree

Mr Sterling Huck
3901 Whitland Ave. #27
Nashville
TN 37205
United States of America

Dear Mr Huck

Re: "The Hourglasses"

Thank you very much for your recent request to trade on our street market this summer.

I am afraid I have to inform you that there is already a trader on our market selling a very similar item, although in their particular case the timetelling equipment is mounted on a range of attractive bracelets and operates either electronically or via a very clever mechanical system. I would therefore suggest that The Hourglasses would not prove popular in Braintree.

Your line of His 'n' Hers Birdbaths was far more tempting as no such items are currently available on our market. However, on consulting the Council's corporate advisors it was pointed out to me that His 'n' Hers Birdbaths contravene the Council's equality policies by being gender exclusive. Perhaps you could consider the feasibility of a unisex alternative.

I would be very interested if you have any further potential items you wish to sell and thank you again for your interest in Braintree street market. It is satisfying to know that our reputation as one of the premier street markets in England is spreading overseas.

Yours sincerely,

Mr. Simon Taylor
Car Parks & Markets Manager

Annie F. Ralph *Chief Executive*

Awarded for
excellence

INVESTOR
IN PEOPLE

FS 28516

March 3, 2002

Fenwick Players
P.O. Box 4044
Kingsport, TN 37664

Dear Fenwick Players,

I'm the world's best "audience finesser." I make angry crowds angrier, happy crowds happier. I ignite and prolong applause. I whip up frenzies of support and delight. I open the floodgate to heartfelt tears. These are just a few of the things I do.

I have an unassuming appearance (I've been told I look a little like the young Dick Cavett, though he didn't wear an eyepatch). I can be subtle, using tricks such as "stealth clapping," or overt, with a raucous, phlegmy laugh. Whatever the situation, I have the tools.

I'd like to offer my services for your upcoming season. I guarantee I can increase ticket sales, stir up controversy and boost overall reaction to your theatrical productions.

I've worked around the world at all kinds of events. You can see me in the best-selling video release *John Tesh Live At Red Rocks*, at approximately 58:03, as I lead a standing ovation for Mr. Tesh.

My rates are reasonable, and we can discuss them at your convenience.

Thank you for your consideration of the "audience finesser." I look forward to hearing from you soon.

Kindest Regards,

Sterling Huck
3901 Whitland Ave. #27
Nashville, TN 37205

Fenwick Players

March 27, 2001

Sterling Huck
3901 Whitland Ave. #27
Nashville, TN 37205

Dear Sterling:

Thank you for your letter and your offer to "finesse" our audiences here at the Fenwick. Unfortunately, I think we'll have to pass. It's the job of our actors, directors, set designers and crew to ignite and prolong applause, and whip up frenzies of support.

But I always did wonder how John Tesh managed to get those standing ovations.

Good luck to you in your career.

Ciao,

Tom Price, Artistic Director
Fenwick Players

January 5, 1998

La-Z-Boy Chair Company
1284 North Telegraph Rd.
Monroe, MI 48162
Attn: Special Orders

Dear La-Z-Boy,

I am a human daredevil named Sterling Huck. In the past decade, I have performed such death-defying feats as scaling The Third National Bank Building in Chattanooga, TN (150 ft.) using only suction cups, walking across three miles of telephone company wire in Hubbard, OH and most recently, being catapulted across the reflecting pool in Washington, D.C. Perhaps you know of this last feat, as it was mentioned on the "20-20" television program with Mr. Hugh Downs.

This spring I am planning my greatest stunt yet, a ride over Niagara Falls in a barrel. I'm writing to you with the fervent hope that your company will design my vessel for this perilous journey. For years, I've enjoyed the comfort and solid construction of my La-Z-Boy recliner and couch, and I can think of no one I'd trust more to build this barrel.

The specs I need are as follows: 4 1/2 feet high, 4 feet in diameter, a waterproof upholstered exterior (maybe in bright canary yellow for maximum visibility), a padded interior with neck and knee braces, and a 100-pound anvil tied to the bottom as an anchor to keep the barrel upright in the rough waters.

As this ride is sure to be a big media event, I would be happy to promote the La-Z-Boy name along with my own skills as a daredevil. I'm currently negotiating with the good folks at Niagara Falls National Park, but my projected date for the barrel ride is May 15, 1998.

Please let me know the costs for constructing the barrel and how long it will take to build. Thank you, and I look forward to your speedy reply!!

Regards,

Sterling Huck

Sterling Huck
3901 Whitland Ave #27
Nashville, TN 37205

LA-Z-BOY®

LA-Z-BOY® INCORPORATED / 1284 N. Telegraph Road, Monroe, Michigan 48162-3390, Phone: (313) 242-1444
FAX: Traffic   (313) 241-2634   FAX: Accounting (313) 241-2635
Advertising (313) 241-4422   Orders   (313) 457-2007

January 19, 1998

Mr. Stirling Huck
3901 Whitland Ave. #27
Nashville, TN 37205

Dear Mr. Huck:

Thank you for your letter of January 5, 1998; it was very interesting reading.

Although we thank you for thinking about us when it comes to comfort and reliability, I believe we will stick with furniture and will pass on your request.

Good Luck.

Sincerely,

Stephen L. Markos
Director, Sales and
Service Administration

SLM/aw

February 7, 2002

Consolidated Pest Control
P.O. Box 307306
Atlanta, GA 30030

DearCPC,

The world will beat a path to the door of the man who can build a better mousetrap, my Uncle Meyer used to say.

Though I always laughed and laughed at Uncle Meyer, I think his credo must've sunk in, because twenty-five years later, I'm writing to you with what I believe is a design for a superior mousetrap, maybe the final word in mousetraps.

As leaders in the field of rodent punishment, I think you'll agree that when we set traditional spring-released "snap traps" we often find the mouse or rat in a messy state - almost severed but not quite, and probably having suffered a long, slow demise. It's unpleasant to see, unpleasant to clean up.

With my "Louis XIV Rodent Guillotine," the capture and execution of these furry pests is easy, clean and decisive (and incisive) in the results.

Modeled after the guillotines used in the court of France's great king, the "Louis XIV Rodent Guillotine" works efficiently and every time. Using a small scrap of food as a lure, the mouse is unwittingly drawn towards the guillotine and through the head bracket, which locks around his neck, then triggers a fast-falling, razor sharp tungsten blade. The mouse is cleanly decapitated, his head dropping into a sturdy metal basket. It's all so simple and humane.

I would like to send a demonstration video for your viewing as soon as possible (see attached picture). Perhaps together we can collaborate on the marketing and sales for the "Louis XIV Rodent Guillotine." Thanks for your consideration.

Kind Regards,

Sterling Huck
3901 Whitland Ave. #27
Nashville, TN 37205

Insects

Consolidated Pest Control

CPC, Inc. P.O. Box 307306, Atlanta, GA 30030 / 404–989–5175

Rodents

February 12, 2002

Sterling Huck
3901 Whitland Ave. #27
Nashville, TN 37205

Dear Mr. Huck,

Thank you for your letter and photo. Although the "Rodent Guillotine" sounds like an effective tool, we'll have to pass. We at Consolidated prefer a more humane approach to dealing with pests and critters.

We wish you all the best with your invention.

Sincerely,

Jim Lash
Executive Controller
CPC, Inc.

February 19, 1998

Mars Incorporated
High Street
Hackettstown, NJ 07840

Dear Mars,

I was excited to hear about the new limited edition "President M & M's" that you'll be offering this year. Will the likenesses of all 41 of our U.S. presidents be featured on the candy shells of M & M's? Or will you be leaving out some of the lesser known presidents, such as Rutherford B. Hayes and Grover Cleveland? I can't wait to see your illustrations of the presidents. It will certainly make me hesitate before I pop a whole handful of chocolate-covered "chiefs of staff" in my mouth!

Will the President M & M's be on both regular and peanut-flavored? I guess the peanut would be easier for your designers to work with, being bigger and all. What does M & M stand for anyways?

If possible I'd like to order some of the "President M & M's" before they come out in stores. I collect presidential stuff. The walls of my room are covered with felt pennants and election posters and I have a drinking mug that looks like the head of LBJ. It's either LBJ or Spiro Agnew, I'm not sure. I don't drink out of it. I keep pencils and paper in it. But I'd like to fill it with "President M & M's," when you make them.

Please send me an order form for "President M & M's" soon. I really love M & M's!

A Happy Customer,

Sterling Huck
3901 Whitland Ave. #27
Nashville, TN 37205

a division of Mars, Incorporated
High Street, Hackettstown, New Jersey 07840 • Telephone 908-852-1000

February 27, 1998

Mr. Sterling Huck
3901 Whitland Ave. #27
Nashville, TN 37205

Dear Mr. Huck:

Thank you for your compliment about "M&M's"® Chocolate Candies. We are
pleased that you enjoy our product and appreciate your taking the time
to tell us so.

The "President M&M's" that you referred to are available to the
President of the United States only.

Please accept the enclosed for a treat with the compliments of M&M/MARS.
It was really nice to hear from you.

Sincerely,

Joanne Vintch
Consumer Affairs

JLV/cl 0903158A

March 7, 2002

The Toro Company
Consumer Division
8111 Lyndale Avenue South
Bloomington, MN 55420

Dear Toro,

There is only one name in the manufacture of lawn mowers, snow blowers
and trimmers, and that's Toro!

That's why I'm turning to you with an idea that I feel certain could
revolutionize the way people live.

Picture this. It's a Saturday afternoon in suburbia. A husband is snoozing in
his favorite easy chair. Suddenly, his wife interrupts his nap and announces
that the grass needs cutting. Grumbling, the man drags himself outside. For
the next two hours he rides, navigating ever-diminishing lawn-shaped
patterns, until the job is done. His shoulders are hunched, his back is sore, his
behind is numb. And all he's thinking about is getting back to that easy chair.
Sound familiar?

Now you can have the best of both worlds with . . . The Yawnmower.

The Yawnmower is a sturdy sit-down tractor-style mower, fully equipped
with an adjustable reclining chair and comfortable headrest. Just set the
steering wheel to automatic pilot, lean back and enjoy the ride. The
Yawnmower does the rest. It's that easy. There's even a drink holder and a
side pouch for salty snacks.

With The Yawnmower you can have your chores and snores together!

I look forward to discussing this idea with you soon.

Kind Regards,

Sterling Huck
3901 Whitland Ave. #27
Nashville, TN 37205

P.S. - What do you think of Dick Butkus as a spokesperson?

The Toro Company

8111 Lyndale Avenue South, Bloomington, Minnesota 55420-1196
• Phone 952/888-8801   • www.toro.com   • Fax 952/887-8258

THE TORO COMPANY POLICY ON OUTSIDE IDEAS

Thank you for taking the time to submit your product related idea to The Toro Company. We sincerely value your interest in Toro.

Following is a summary of The Toro Company policy on outside ideas:

1. Toro evaluates all ideas relating to its field of business if the idea is covered by an **issued** United States "utility" patent. Your U.S. patent is a "utility" patent if it has a seven digit "patent number", e.g., 4,925,233.

2. If the outside idea is covered by an issued United States utility patent, the inventor and/or patent owner should submit a photocopy of the <u>complete issued patent</u> to:

> Outside Idea Coordinator
> The Toro Company
> 8111 Lyndale Avenue South
> Bloomington, MN 55420

3. Other than giving us your name and address and a copy of your patent, <u>do not</u> send any additional materials or information. The patent should be self-explanatory. If you submit or have already submitted materials other than an issued United States patent, these materials are being or will be returned to you. If you have already submitted an issued United States patent, it will be evaluated pursuant to this policy. The patent will not be returned to you. We do not photocopy or retain any materials that you submit to us other than issued United States patents.

4. Toro will review the patent and will contact the inventor and/or patent owner <u>only if Toro is interested in acquiring rights to the technology disclosed in the patent</u>.

As always, if you have a problem or a concern with a Toro product that you own and/or operate, you should contact the dealer or distributor through which the product was purchased.

Again, we thank you for considering The Toro Company and we wish you success in marketing your idea.

October 31, 2001

Yellow Cab Company
P.O. Box 174621
Memphis, TN 38117

Dear Yellow Cab,

These are troubled times for foreign cab drivers. Though they may be upstanding citizens of our great country, possible fares may eye them with suspicion.

That's why I've developed the "Inst-American" kit for cabbies. With the help of this easy to use multi-media kit, your drivers can go from baba ghanough to apple pie in minutes, stepping up their patriotism and stepping up your business!

Included in the "Inst-American" kit:

- A mix tape with 90 minutes of all-American favorites such as "God Bless America" by Kate Smith, "God Bless The USA" by Lee Greenwood, "America The Beautiful" by Jim Nabors, "Born In The USA" by Bruce Springsteen, "R.O.C.K. In The U.S.A." by John Cougar, "The Caissons Go Rolling Along" by Sgt. Walt Wilkins & Friends, plus lots more.

- A red, white and blue stovepipe hat (made from sturdy Dura-Mold, one size fits all)

- An assortment of flags, banners and streamers to decorate the interior of the cab

- A pocket-size book of Major League Baseball trivia

- A glossary of all-American sayings, such as "Now you're talkin', buddy," "You and me both, pal," "Hey, don't I know it!" "Hits you right where you live, don't it?" and more.

- Instructions on how to give the "Inst-American" healing touch to dispirited customers

I can send you one sample "Inst-American" kit for 7 days trial use, free of charge. Try it on one of your drivers. If you're not convinced return it to me, no questions asked.

It's time for the "Inst-American." Its truth goes marching on!

Kind Regards,

Sterling Huck
3901 Whitland Ave. #27
Nashville, TN 37205
US of A

Yellow Cab Company
901-9YE-LLOW / 901-993-5569

November 7, 2001

Sterling Huck
3901 Whitland Ave. #27
Nashville, TN 37205

Dear Mr. Huck,

Thank you for your interest in employment opportunities with Yellow Cab Company.

Please call Don Donahue at 901-993-5569 to discuss the matter further.

Sincerely,

Bill Clark
Yellow Cab Company

February 24, 1997

General Electric
3135 Easton Turnpike
Fairfield, CT 06431
Attn: New Product Ideas

Dear Sirs,

I'm an inventor with a keen interest in all things electric. Over the years, I've secured patents on many of my ideas and innovations, such as the **Clapper Disc** (a CD player with a built-in clapper), the **Dashboard Toast-R-Oven** and the **Mariner Chewing Gum** (fish-flavored gum).

Recently, I've been tinkering with lightbulbs. Starting from the premise that most of us are usually surprised when bulbs burn out and we're caught without a replacement, I've developed the perfect solution: a bulb that keeps us updated on its lifespan.

Imagine flipping on a light switch and hearing a voice say "Seventy-four hours left" or "Three hours and twenty minutes left, time for a new bulb." It's all possible with my new invention, **The Bantering Bulb.** It's novel, fun and economical. I'm even working on a variation, an energy saver that would reprimand wasteful family members with a gruff warning of "Hey you, I'm burning up in here!" This model will be called **The Raging Bulb.** It might even have a New York accent.

Fitting each bulb with my special voice-activated meter costs only a few cents more, and I have a hunch that, with proper ad campaigns, this idea could electrify the industry (imagine a line of "celebrity bulbs." For example, Jonathan Harris, the voice of Dr. Smith from Lost In Space, saying "Oh dear, oh dear, only five minutes left!)

Thanks for your consideration of **The Bantering Bulb** and **The Raging Bulb.**

Best Regards,

Sterling Huck
3901 Whitland Ave. #27
Nashville, TN 37205

Margaret M. Todd
Manager
Submitted Ideas

General Electric Company
3135 Easton Turnpike, Fairfield, CT 06431
203 373-2449

March 19, 1997

Mr. Sterling Huck
3901 Whitland Avenue, #17
Nashville, TN 37205

Dear Mr. Huck:

This is in response to your February 24, 1997, letter. Thank you for your interest in General Electric Company.

We are pleased to have you think of our Company in connection with your idea relating to the light bulbs.

Before you disclose your idea to us, however, we feel that you should carefully read the enclosed booklet, "Consideration of Submitted Ideas," and particularly the terms concerning submissions which appear on pages 1, 2 and 12 of the booklet.

If you then find either of the two suggested bases of submission acceptable, please select and fill out the appropriate form provided in the booklet and return it to us with a description of your idea. Upon its receipt we shall be very happy to consider your proposal.

Very truly yours,

Margaret M. Todd

Enclosure

MMT:rbp

June 17, 1998

Smithsonian Institution
1000 Jefferson Dr. SW
Washington, DC 20560

To The Smithsonian,

I have been attending professional hockey games for over thirty-two years and in that time I have collected the teeth of many well-known NHL players. Hockey, as you know, is a rough sport, with sticks slicing, pucks flying and bodies being checked into the boards. Many players lose their teeth. And I have them.

Some of the teeth in my collection (all have been verified by a dentist, Dr. Rudolph Lars) include: Rod Gilbert, Bobby Orr, Stan Mikita, Guy Lafleur, Jean Ratelle, Mark Messier and Luc Robitalle. I have one of the legendary Gordie Howe's incisors that I bought from another collector. Also I have numerous fillings, bonds, mouthguards and veneers.

 I would like to offer this fascinating display of NHL players' teeth to your museum for an exhibit (maybe we could call it something like "Molars On Ice"). Please let me know when I can send you a photographic catalog of the teeth.

Thanks for your consideration. I look forward to hearing from you.

Kind Regards,

Sterling Huck
3901 Whitland Ave. #27
Nashville, TN 37205

The Smithsonian did not feel this would be a crowd-pleasing exhibit.

Sterling is currently considering an offer from The Museum of Extracted Wisdom Teeth in Wylertown, Pennsylvania.

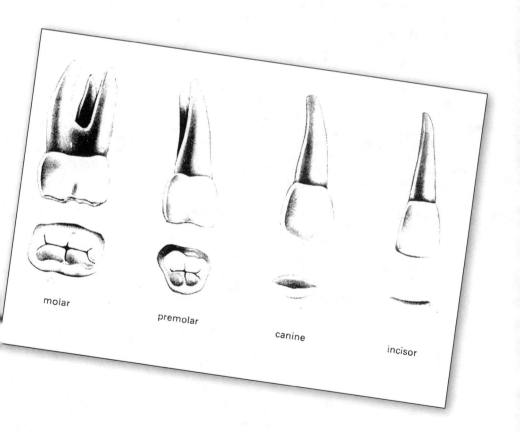

molar

premolar

canine

incisor

January 10, 2002

Beholder Eyewear
3 St. Martin Lane
London WC1 3EE
England

Dear Beholder,

I have an idea that I believe could start a new trend in eyewear for your company. It's called the "Sunocle."

Based on the monocle, the single eyeglass that was so popular in the latter part of the 19th century, especially among the aristocracy in Europe, the "Sunocle" would give a person the opportunity to experience a beautiful sunny day with one tinted eye and one naked eye. So often, I feel that sunglasses can compromise the view of the natural world by adding unwanted shades and hues. With the "Sunocle" that problem would be solved.

From a fashion standpoint, I think the single tinted circular lens with a nylon cord attached (and these could be done in day–glo colors) would catch on big with young people. Remember Werner Klemperer, who played Colonel Klink on *Hogan's Heroes*? Very popular with young people. I've heard that Hollywood is doing a big screen remake of *Hogan's Heroes*, so perhaps there could be some advertising tie-in. Other great monocle wearers from America's past include Teddy Roosevelt, Lionel Barrymore, Rudy Vallee, Nelson Rockefeller and Mark Spitz (the Olympic champ liked to swim with a monogoggle).

Thank you for consideration of my idea. I would be glad to work with your researchers on it. After all, two heads are better than one, but one lens is better than two!

Kindest Regards,

Sterling Huck

Sterling Huck
3901 Whitland Ave. #27
Nashville, TN 37205
USA

beholder eyewear

visionary fashion design

11 February 2002

Sterling Huck
3901 Whitland Ave. #27
Nashville, TN 37204

Re: "The Sunocle"

Dear Sterling,

Thank you for your comments about Beholder Eyewear. It's always a pleasure to hear from our customers.

The many aspects of our design and production are under constant review, with the intention of making improvements wherever possible. The opinions of our customers play a crucial role in that process, and we appreciate you taking the time to send us yours.

Your letter will be forwarded to the appropriate personnel for evaluation.

Best Regards,

Bettina Driscoll
Customer Relations

February 26, 1997

Hasbro
200 Narragansett Park Drive
Pawtucket, RI 02862

Dear Hasbro,

I'm an independent toy maker, best known for my game, *Ker-Fluffle, The Dunk Tank Clown*, which sold nearly 15,000 units in Europe last year. I've also developed such toys as *Daddy Bob's Miniature Chicken Farm* and *The Homestead Act: Official Play Set*. Beyond that, I was a designer on the popular amusement park ride, *Captain Hernia's Magic Hammer*.

I'm about to unveil a new line of Jack-In-The-Box toys that I think will be extremely popular with children and adults of all ages. I would love to work with your company on developing them. It's an updating of a perennial favorite toy.

Here's what I'm working on:

Monterey Jack-In-The-Box - A big, tasty slab of cheese on a spring. Catch it with a cracker, or a hamburger!

Jack Ruby-In-The-Box - Relive one of history's most gruesome moments of revenge (Lee Harvey Oswald not included).

Freejack-In-The-Box - Mick Jagger, thespian, in a sci-fi classic. Nuff said.

Jack Nicklaus In-The-Box - The Golden Bear is caught in a sandtrap on the 18th hole. Will he get out? Open the lid! (Sand included)

Billy Jack-In-The-Box - Equal rights for Native Americans and a karate chop! (boots are removable)

Jack Klugman-In-The-Box - Everyone's favorite sloppy sportswriter comes out covered in beer foam and snack chips.

Jack Lord In-The-Box - The return of Steve McGarrett. Book 'em Dan-O!!

Jack The Ripper-In-The-Box - Don't get too close to this one!

Thanks for your consideration of my idea. I look forward to hearing from you soon.

Kind Regards,

Sterling Huck
3901 Whitland Ave. #27
Nashville, TN 37205

March 5, 1997

MR. STERLING HUCK
3901 WHITLAND AVE. #27
NASHVILLE, TN 37205

Dear MR. HUCK,

Thank you for contacting The Hasbro Toy Group regarding a new
product idea. We appreciate your interest in our company.

As you can imagine, each year we receive many contacts and inquiries
such as yours, and while we appreciate hearing from our friends and
consumers, we must advise you that we do not accept unsolicited
submissions for review.

In accordance with our policy, we are enclosing the material you
sent to us, which we have neither copied nor reviewed. We wish you
well with your efforts.

Sincerely,

HASBRO CONSUMER AFFAIRS DEPARTMENT

HASBRO, INC.   200 Narragansett Park Drive, P.O. Box 200, Pawtucket, RI 02862–0200 USA (401) 431-8697

November 7, 1995   **NO REPLY**

Transcience Corporation
Home of the Sea Monkey
P.O. Box 809
Bryans Road, MD 20616

Dear Transcience,

I'm an independent filmmaker, known best for my science fiction underground classic *Get Larry Laser!* (starring Roy Clark and Indigo Matahi). Currently, I'm in the development stages for my next picture, tentatively titled *Attack Of The Giant Sea Monkey.* I'm in talks with Russ Tamblyn to play the part of Mark Ryan, the heroic scientist. Art Garfunkel is my second choice.

Knowing that your company is the foremost authority on the sea monkey, I wondered if you could help me with the problem of designing my monster - a huge sea monkey! It would be roughly 30 feet tall and weigh over 5,000 pounds. Could you possibly provide a rough sketch for me or at least a detailed description of the giant sea monkey? I plan to construct it out of paper mache and plastic milk jugs.

Also, is the sea monkey carnivorous?

Thank you for your help. You will receive a mention in the credits of *Attack Of The Giant Sea Monkey.* I look forward to hearing from you.

Regards,

Sterling Huck
3901 Whitland Ave. #27
Nashville, TN 37205

October 21, 2001

NO REPLY

Endust
3 First National Plaza
Chicago, IL 60602
Attn: Consumer Relations

Dear Endust,

I read with great interest in the September issue of *Beautiful Furniture Magazine* about your new polish called Zendust.

As a long time meditator and Buddhist dabbler, I immediately jotted down some possible catchphrases for your advertising campaign. Feel free to use any of the following:

The question, "What is too much dust?"
The answer, "Exactly."

One spray of Zendust and dust is no longer dust. After awhile, dust is once again dust.

It's a fundamental delusion to consider that the dust is covering something that's more important than the dust itself.

Spray once, be connected. Spray twice, be rejected. Spray three times, be enlightened.

Thank you. I can't wait to try new Zendust. When does it hit the shelves of my supermarket?

Yours in Peace,

Sterling Huck

Sterling Huck
3901 Whitland Ave. #27
Nashville, TN 37205

November 6, 2001

Harrod's
87 Brompton Rd.
London SW1X JXL
England

Dear Harrod's,

I am America's foremost sculptor of roadside Gorilla statues.

Though I'm probably best known for The Mattress Warehouse "Mandrill" (nine stores throughout the southeast) and the Firestorm Tires "Quality Gibbon" (Joelton, TN), I've designed and built over 900 roadside gorillas. The actor Scott Baio has purchased three of my gorillas. And Sammy Hagar has one.

Whether shopping for tires or donuts or mattresses, people love to see a gorilla out in front of a store. It gives them a warm feeling, and it's a sign of high quality. Studies show that storefront gorillas increase business by up to 31% in the first three months.

Maybe you've never thought about it, but Harrod's could benefit from having a gorilla. I'm envisioning your gorilla at about 7-feet tall, 200 lbs. (plastimold over a metal frame). He will be a mighty alpha male with clenched fists poised over leathery black pectorals. He'll have blazing amber eyes and an angry sneer. For extra, I can wire in a voice box that enables the gorilla to say, "Welcome to Harrod's" or maybe just let out a savage cry.

I'm ready to start making your gorilla today! Thanks for your consideration. I look forward to hearing from you.

Kind Regards,

Sterling Huck
3901 Whitland Ave. #27
Nashville, TN 37205
USA

**In the grand old British tradition,
Harrod's essentially said, "Good Lord,
man, have you lost your mind?"**

September 4, 1998

Merriam Webster Co.
P.O. Box 281
Springfield, MA 01102

Dear Webster's,

I use your dictionaries everyday! If I'm searching for the meaning of a word, I'll open my New Collegiate. There's no substitute. Just yesterday a fellow remarked on a hat I was wearing. "That's a nice cap, but with all this sun, it's too bad it doesn't have a havelock," he said. "Havelock"? I'd never heard the word, but you provided me with the definition: "a covering attached to a cap to protect the neck from the sun or bad weather."

The reason I'm writing is that I have two new words that I think you might want to add to your next dictionary. The first is "greetnot." It's a noun for that unacknowledged gesture that begins as a wave and ends as a rubbing of the nose or the back of the head. Like in this sentence: "Sherry turned the corner a second too soon, and Jack's friendly wave sagged into a greetnot." It could also be a verb, as in "Jack greetnotted Sherry." I think it's a valuable word that would do well in your dictionary.

The other word is "verbalimbo." It's for those times when you find yourself saying, "Bu. . ., I . . . Ca . . . .," trying to get a word in edgewise. "Caught between the rapid fire volley of Spanish cursing of his mother-in-law and wife, Pedro was in verbalimbo for ten minutes."

These words are free of charge. But maybe I could get a discount on my next dictionary purchase, or you could give me a credit (in parentheses) after each entry for these words. I hope you can use them in your next dictionary.

Whatever happened to the word "spuddle"?

Best Regards,

Sterling Huck
3901 Whitland Ave. #27
Nashville, TN 37205

Merriam Webster

From the Inkwell to the Internet

September 16, 1998

Sterling Huck
3901 Whitland Avenue, #27
Nashville, TN 37205

Dear Mr. Huck:

We have your letter in which you submit for our consideration as dictionary entries the coinages *greetnot* and *verbalimbo*.

We appreciate your verbal creativity, and we're going to add these coinages to our new words file. However, we should tell you that new words are not automatically added to the dictionary. Before we can enter a new term in the dictionary, we need to collect evidence of the use of the term by several different writers over a period of a few years. This evidence consists of examples of the term's use in print —newspapers, books, magazines, circulars, etc. These examples are necessary because many new words fail to catch on and thus do not warrant entry in the dictionary. If you should come across any occurrences of these coinages in print, we'd be happy to add them to our files.

The verb *spuddle*, while not an entry in our *Collegiate Dictionary*, is included in our unabridged *Webster's Third New International Dictionary*. It is labeled *archaic* because we have very little evidence of its use in this century. It was used to mean "to stir up liquid" or "to dig up earth superficially."

Thank you for your interest in our dictionaries.

Sincerely yours,

James G. Lowe

JGL/gbb

Merriam-Webster Inc.
47 Federal Street • P.O. Box 281 • Springfield, MA 01102
Telephone (413) 734-3134 • Facsimile (413) 731-5979 • http://www.m-w.com

150 Years of Excellence

August 17, 1996

NO REPLY

Panasonic Corporation
One Panasonic Way
Secaucus, NJ 07094

Dear Sirs,

I've recently purchased one of your CLP-128 CD players with "The Clapper" built in. As a man who sometimes has difficulty breathing, I appreciate the convenience of being able to remain in my chair, and with a clap of my hands, turn on my favorite music.

There is a small problem, however, in that the CLP-128 can't always distinguish between recorded claps and real ones. For example, if I play "I Want To Hold Your Hand" by The Beatles or "High Heeled Sneakers" by Stevie Wonder, the recorded handclaps will shut the player off. Even worse is my Buddy Greco *Live At The Sands* CD, a recording punctuated by frequent applause. I'm still looking forward to hearing his "weather report" medley of "Sunny," "Windy" and "Here's That Rainy Day," but thus far, I have been unable to.

I've tried listening at lower volumes but it doesn't seem to help. I'd like to enjoy my Panasonic CLP-128 to the fullest. Any suggestions?

Regards,

Sterling Huck
3901 Whitland Ave. #27
Nashville, TN 37205

Opportunity Knocks

June 1, 2001

Office of the City Manager
201 West Gray
Norman, OK 73069

Dear Norman City Manager,

I want to open a moustache wax superstore in Norman. It will be called
Baron von Snickerdoodle's Moustache Wax Emporium. I'll sell imported
moustache wax, moustache combs and a variety of shaving equipment. We
may also carry "stage moustaches."

An independent study from the ATA (American Tonsorial Assocation) showed
that there were more men with moustaches in Oklahoma than any other
state in the country! Think about all the people you know with moustaches.

I have investors and a team of employees ready to relocate to Norman. How's
the market for homes there? Please send me the necessary paperwork to
launch Baron von Snickerdoodle's Moustache Wax Emporium.

Thank you very much.

Kind Regards,

Sterling Huck
3901 Whitland Ave. #27
Nashville, TN 37205

P.S. - I have a commitment from baseball legend and moustache wax endorser
Sal Bando to sign autographs on opening day!

The City of
NORMAN
201 WEST GRAY • P.O. BOX 370
NORMAN, OKLAHOMA 73070

OFFICE OF THE CITY CLERK
(405) 366-5406

June 6, 2001

Mr. Sterling Huck
3901 Whitland Avenue #27
Nashville, Tennessee 37205

Dear Mr. Huck:

I received your letter dated June 1, 2001, regarding your desire to open a moustache wax superstore in Norman. The City of Norman, Oklahoma, does not require a business license for the selling of shaving related equipment. You will need a sales tax permit number which you can request from the Oklahoma Tax Commission by calling 405-521-3279 or writing them at 2501 North Lincoln, Connors Building, Oklahoma City, Oklahoma, 73105-4396.

In regards to the housing market in Norman you may want to contact the Chamber of Commerce through their website, normanok.org, or write them at Post Office Box 982, Norman, Oklahoma, 73070, or phone them at 405-321-7260.

I hope this information is helpful and if you need anything further, please feel free to contact me.

Sincerely,

Mary Hatley
City Clerk

smr

February 4, 1998

Sears, Roebuck & Co.
3333 Beverly Rd.
Hoffman Estates, IL 60179

Dear Sears,

I am a multi-linguist, with a special interest in arcane languages. As a translator I have published hundreds of best-selling books, including the Somali version of Erich Segal's *Love Story*, the Armenian translation of *Merv: An Autobiography*, and most recently, the Fang-Bulu release of Robert James Waller's *The Bridges Of Madison County*.

Because I'm deeply in love with languages, even in my spare time I find that I'm translating whatever's in front of me. As a fun project, I've recently been translating the new Sears catalog into Old Saxon. It's a challenge, I can tell you, especially since this grand old tongue does not have words for undergarments.

As I enjoy spending time leafing through your handsome catalog, I'd like to know if you'd be interested in hiring me on as a translator. It could be an opportunity to have your merchandise reach whole new customers! Imagine a Sears catalog in Berber or Uzbek!

I look forward to hearing from you soon.

Regards,

Sterling Huck
3901 Whitland Ave. #27
Nashville, TN 37205

Sears Merchandise Group
3333 Beverly Road
Hoffman Estates, IL   60179
(847)286-5188
                                              February 12, 1998

Sterling Huck
3901 WHITLAND AVE. # 27
NASHVILLE, TN.   37205

Case Number: 31502453

Dear Sterling Huck:

Your recent letter addressed to SEARS ROEBUCK has been directed
to Sears National Customer Relations for response. We would
like to sincerely apologize for any inconvenience this
situation may have caused you.

We would like to be able to assist you further, but need your
telephone number in order to do so. Please provide us with
your phone number or contact our office at your earliest
convenience at (847) 286-5188 and one of our Customer
Relations Representatives will be available to assist you.

Thank you for taking the time to write us and for bringing this
matter to our attention.

National Customer Relations

043023001

September 20, 1999

Amoco
200 East Randolph Dr. MC 3408
Chicago, IL 60601

Dear Amoco,

I'm planning to open a chain of stores around the south central U.S. and the name I intend to use for my franchise is "Hamoco." I'll be selling cured hams, pork salted hams, aged Virginia hams, hamhocks, ham sandwiches, ham jerky - anything to do with ham, I'll have it! Studies show that ham is a popular meat in the south.

I know the name Hamoco is slightly reminiscent of Amoco, but I won't be selling any gasoline or motor oil. My store logo is a red, white and blue oval (roughly in the shape of a canned ham) with bold black lettering that says Hamoco.

I plan to open the first Hamoco in Birmingham, Alabama in February 2000, so I thought I'd let you know about it. Thanks for your support.

By the way, whenever I can, I always fuel up at Amoco. It's the best thing for my car!

Regards,

Sterling Huck
P.O. Box 92034
Nashville, TN 37209

Robert E. Blankenbaker
Attorney

BP Amoco Corporation

Law Department
Mail Code 2002B
200 East Randolph Drive
Post Office Box 87703 (60680-0703)
Chicago, Illinois 60601-7125
312-856-2054
Facsimile: 312-856-6798
Email: blankere@bp.com

October 7, 1999

Mr. Sterling Huck
P.O. Box 92034
Nashville, TN 37209

Dear Mr. Huck:

Your letter of September 20, 1999 has reached my desk. I handle trademark
matters for BP Amoco Corporation. While your description of the Hamoco logo
makes it sound quite different than the world famous Amoco Torch & Oval logo,
we would like to review the Hamoco graphics. Can you provide us with a color
copy of the proposed graphics?

Very truly yours,

Robert E. Blankenbaker

REB/tw

October 13, 1999

Robert E. Blankenbaker
BP Amoco Corporation
Law Dept.
Mail Code 2002B
200 East Randolph Dr.
P.O. Box 87703
Chicago, IL 60601-7125

Dear Mr. Blankenbaker,

Thank you for your letter of October 7, 1999. As per your request, I'm sending the "Hamoco" logo. This is the rough sketch I submitted to the graphic design company, so please forgive the crudeness of the shape (it's supposed to look like a canned ham!) and the lettering. When Mr. Matahi, the designer, is finished, it will be beautiful. I think you'll agree that besides perhaps a similarity in coloring, it's quite different from the famous Amoco Torch & Oval logo.

In my previous letter, I think I mentioned February 2000 as a target date for the grand opening of the first Hamoco store. June may be a more realistic date now, due to the problems I've been having with my back (I threw it out lifting a 170-lb. Virginia ham). Business is difficult to conduct in the supine position.

Please let me know if there are any ham products you and your family enjoy, and I'll be sure to send a special "Hamoco Hello Basket" your way.

Thanks for your support. Please let me know if there's anything else you need.

Kind Regards,

Sterling Huck
P.O. Box 92034
Nashville, TN 37209

this is a rough sketch . . . .

note: a small pig's
head may be attached
to the top of the
"canned ham" sign . . . .

Red →
White →
Blue →

* the sign will rotate . . .

© 1999 Huck

Robert E. Blankenbaker
Attorney

BP Amoco Corporation

Law Department
Mail Code 2002B
200 East Randolph Drive
Post Office Box 87703 (60680-0703)
Chicago, Illinois 60601-7125

312-856-2054
Facsimile: 312–856-6798
Email: blankere@bp.com

November 22, 1999

Mr. Sterling Huck
P.O. Box 92034
Nashville, TN 37209

Dear Mr. Huck:

Thank you for your recent letter along with the proposed graphics. I asked our marketing people to review the proposed signage. There is some concern that the combination of "Hamoco" with a red, white and blue oval might lead to a portion of the public believing that "Hamoco" is somehow related to Amoco. Accordingly, they would like to see either the name or the color scheme changed in order to create a greater separation between Amoco signage and Hamoco signage. Thank you for giving us an opportunity to review the proposed graphics.

Very truly yours,

Bob

Robert E. Blankenbaker

REB/tw

Date: Tuesday, November 30, 1999 8:06:50 PM
Subj: Hamoco Logo
To: blankere@bp.com

Dear Mr. Blankenbaker,

Thank you for your letter of November 22, 1999. I'm recovering from my back injury, but it's still slow going in the planning of the Hamoco franchise. I do have a computer with internet capabilities now though.

I understand your concerns about my proposed sign. I showed the rough drawing to a few complete strangers and asked them what it reminded them of. Almost all said, "Amoco Gasoline." Aw heck, that's going to be a problem, I thought. I want my company to have an individual image.

One idea I had was to recast the oval as the bold outline of a large pig, still retaining the red, white and blue stripes with the black lettering. It may still be too similar. What do you think?

Another idea is to keep the oval, but change the name. A few I'm considering:

Hamocon
HamWay
Rumpleshankskin
Pig 66
Pork N' Spoon
Ham Hucks (that one would get my name in there)
Kenny Rogers Ham Shop (I'd have to approach him about lending his name, of course. Do you know him?)

If you have any opinions on these company names, I'd be glad to hear them. In the meantime, I'll tell my graphic designer to hold off on the logo (Hamoco in the red, white and blue oval).

Sorry for any confusion. I look forward to hearing from you.

Best Regards,

Sterling Huck

Date: Thursday, December 2, 1999 11:31:46 AM
From: BlankeRE@bp.com
Subj: RE: Hamoco Logo
To: Sterlhuck@aol.com

Dear Sterling,

Thank you for your recent e-mail. I can emphathize with your back pain -- I am walking around at half mast today due to a muscle spasm in my back. Hope you recover soon.

My guess is that either changing the oval to a pig design or changing the name would likely avoid any problem. I guess I would like to see whatever you come up with. Please keep me posted.

By the way, being a native Virginian, you may not find it surprising that my favorite food group is barbequed pork.

Best Regards,

Bob

- - - - - - - - - -

January 31, 1997

NO REPLY

Kiwi Brands Inc.
447 Old Swede Rd.
Douglassville, PA 19518-1239

Dear Kiwi,

In these politically correct times, I have what might be deemed the most "incorrect"
occupation in the country. I'm the president of Tambones & Company, a traveling troupe
of blackface performers. Our intent is in no way to poke fun at African-Americans or
people of color, but rather to preserve the great vaudeville minstrel tradition of singin' and
dancin'. As the immortal Al Jolson once said, "Let me sing a nation's popular songs and
dance my way into their hearts - and then I'll be happy!" Our sentiments exactly!

After years of experimentation, we've found that your brand of shoe polish is the most
effective make-up for blackface performing. The reason I'm writing is to ask if you might
be willing to underwrite our next tour, which begins in May '97. It will be carrying us
through seven southern states with over forty dates. In exchange for your support, of
course, we will promote your product on all our stops, and appear in any magazine or
television ads you'd like. We're quite a talented bunch! Our piano player, Skeets, has
even written a little jingle called "Shine Of The Times" that might interest you.

In any event, I look forward to having Tambones & Company join forces with Kiwi.
Please advise us of your position regarding this matter.

Yowzah,

Sterling Huck
3901 Whitland Ave. #27
Nashville, TN 37205

August 26, 1996

Oriental Institute Museum
1155 E. 58th St.
Chicago, IL

Dear Sirs,

I'm an independent producer, currently scouting for a home setting for a new cable TV cooking program called MUMMY CHEF.

As you probably know, cooking shows are quite popular these days and with so many of them on the air, you have to have a twist, or a gimmick, if you will.

Actor/culinary wizard Ramses Needlebaum and myself have created what we feel is an intriguing, innovative concept in cooking shows. In brief, the MUMMY CHEF, played by Ramses (wrapped in gauze and muslin bandages), offers exotic recipes culled from ancient cookbooks - Egyptian, Greek and Roman. There's everything from "Pharaoh's Chicken" to "Yak Marinara." There will also be special effects such as smoke machines and lasers, along with a blend of middle-Eastern and rock music, to give the show atmosphere.

Is it possible we may be able to film a pilot for the MUMMY CHEF at your museum? I feel the setting would be perfect. You would of course receive a strong plug on the cooking program, as well as free advertising (and lunch!)

Thank you for your consideration. Ramses and I look forward to hearing from you.

Best Regards,

Sterling Huck
3901 Whitland Ave. #27
Nashville, TN 37205

THE ORIENTAL INSTITUTE MUSEUM
THE UNIVERSITY OF CHICAGO
1155 EAST 58TH STREET
CHICAGO · ILLINOIS 60637-1569 U.S.A.

Mr. Sterling Huck
3901 Whitland Avenue #27
Nashville, TN 37205

Sept. 29, 1996

TEL: (312) 702-9520
FAX: (312) 702-9853

Dear Mr. Huck,

Thank you for your letter of August 26 inquiring about the possibility of using the galleries of the Oriental Institute Museum as a setting for your proposed "Mummy Chef" program.

The galleries are closed for renovation until Spring 1998, and thus are inaccessible. In any event, there would not be any possibility of actually cooking in our gallery due to the fire hazard, the smoke and the humidity which the process would produce. I suspect that you will hear a similar judgment from any other museum that you contact.

If you indeed proceed with the project, you may wish to consider a setting other than a museum; perhaps using the pyramid in Memphis as a backdrop, or you may wish to contact Jim Onan the owner of the "Pyramid House" in Wadsworth Illinois (about an hour north of Chicago).

How do you get tomato stains off mummy wrappings?

Good luck with the project.

Sincerely,

Emily Teeter, Ph.D.
Assistant Curator

April 22, 2002

Al Gore
c/o Middle Tennessee State University
1301 East Main Street
Murfreesboro, TN 37132-0001

Dear Mr. Gore,

I am the president of Neckties For Peace, a small non-profit organization based in Nashville, Tennessee. To be honest, there is only one member of NFP, and that's me. But I think once I get going, it will gain in membership.

To do my part in promoting peaceful global relations, I am sending all important leaders around the world a necktie and asking them to autograph it. Once I have received all the signed ties, I will exhibit them at galleries and museums around the United States.

Thanks for participating! Please tell your political colleagues about Neckties For Peace.

I wish you all the best.

Kind Regards,

Sterling Huck
3901 Whitland Ave. #27
Nashville, TN 37205

P.S. - I voted for you in the last election.

2000
Election
Night
Victory
Celebration

NOV. 7, 2000
PHILADELPHIA
P A

May 5, 2001

Wise Potato Chips
180 E. Broad St.
Columbus, OH 43215

Dear Wisemen,

I come from a long line of town criers. My great, great grandfather, Benjamin J. Huck, was the town crier who broke the sad news in Washington, DC about President McKinley's assassination by Anton Czolgosch.

These days, with daily newspapers, CNN and internet news, there's not much need for a town crier of the "topical" kind. Nevertheless, I've found a way to carry on my family tradition. I travel from town to town with a simple mission: to spread the good word about Wise Potato Chips. I love your potato chips! So far, I've been on busy corners in Murfreesboro, TN, Bowling Green, KY and many towns in Ohio, including Blue Ash, Struthers and Hubbard, putting the world "Wise," so to speak.

I use a megaphone (not the battery-operated kind, but the one favored by old-time crooners such as Freddie Moon), and I shout / sing, "Wise Potato Chips taste great!" "Get Wise . . . (3 second pause) . . . Potato Chips!" or "Hoot-hoot-hoot, the Wise Owl says potato chips improve your sex life!" And so on.

Passersby seem to enjoy my crying, especially when I offer them a Wise potato chip from my large owl-shaped front pack. I have been asked by mounted policemen to move on a few times because I didn't possess a license for "town crying." Once in Columbus, I spent three hours in a jail cell, but the good "Wise" name was my passkey out.

I'd love to attend your next Wise Potato Chip convention, to greet employees from the fifty states. In the meantime, I'll be crying for Wise in towns across America!

Regards,

Sterling Huck
3901 Whitland Ave. #27
Nashville, TN 37205

Wise thanked Sterling for being such a
good customer and offered him two
"hush coupons" to stop his crying.

WISE FOODS, INC.
Consumer Affairs Department
228 Raseley Street
Berwick, PA 18603

Mr. Sterling Huck
#27
3901 Whitland Ave
Nashville, TN 37205

September 10, 1998

Willowbrook Mall
1400 Willowbrook Mall
Wayne, NJ 07470

Dear Willowbrook,

I am a professional sketch artist and soon I'll be moving to your area. For years, I was a popular fixture at the shopping malls of middle Tennessee. Unlike other sketch artists who render mall customers in somber profile, soft pastels or exaggerated caricatures, I have my own unique approach.

Using a large sheet of paper sectioned off into quadrants, I depict each subject at four different ages. Square One is how they looked as a small child. Square Two is the young adult. Square Three the middle-aged adult. And Square Four (which is particularly fascinating to the younger customers) is what I call the "death mask," or how they will look in their final repose. Of course, depending on the age of the sitter, I can extrapolate backwards or forwards.

These drawings of mine, which I call "Quads," have been extremely popular, and have drawn lots of extra business to shopping malls. I've even done a few celebrities - Scott Baio and Jenny McCarthy (even in Quad Four, her mouth was open wide).

I'd like to offer my services exclusively to your mall. Please let me know about availability of space and what you charge for rental.

Thank you for your consideration.

Kind Regards,

Sterling Huck
3901 Whitland Ave. #27
Nashville, TN 37205

W I L L O W B R O O K

September 24, 1998

Mr. Sterling Huck
3901 Whitland Ave. #27
Nashville, TN 37205

Dear Sterling:

We are in receipt of your request for temporary space in the marketplace program at Willowbrook Mall. At the present time, we are not looking to expand our market with your merchandise category.

Should we find the category becomes desirable and a location is suitable, consideration may be given to your request.

Please do not hesitate to contact me should you have another concept you are interested in pursuing.

Thank you for your interest in Willowbrook Mall.

Sincerely,

Doreen Jolly
Manager, Specialty Retail

srspace

WILLOWBROOK MANAGEMENT CORPORATION
1400 WILLOWBROOK MALL
WAYNE, NEW JERSEY 07470
TEL: 973 785 1655
FAX: 973 785 8632

February 2, 2002

Royal Canadian Egg Board
Consumer Services
9223 S.W. Marine Drive
Vancouver, BC V6J 1Z4
Canada

Dear Royal Canadian Egg,

I'm an Easter Egg psychic. For years, I have been helping people of all ages find eggs that have been either too cleverly hidden or lost. I work from physical clues. Maybe it's a few pieces of colored straw from an Easter basket, or maybe it's the Paas copper wire contraption that was used to dip the eggs in dye. Whatever it is, it enables me to see the missing egg, visualize its environment, then track it down, with unerring accuracy.

I'm like the Amazing Kreskin, but with eggs. I also work with egg salad and egg cremes, but not reliably.

I would like to make my services available to you and your members (in my experience, farmers have been distrustful of my abilities). How can I advertise in your Egg Board bulletin?

I should mention that I was even consulted in the famous case of the blue peregrine falcon eggs, stolen from the Atlanta Zoo in 1997.

My motto is "Cracking cases, not shells." Thank you for your help. I look forward to working with you.

Regards,

Sterling Huck
3901 Whitland Ave. #27
Nashville, TN 37205

Royal Canadian Egg Board
Consumer Services
9223 S.W. Marine Drive
Vancouver, B.C. V6J 1Z4

23 February 2002

Sterling Huck
3901 Whitland Ave. #27
Nashville, Tennessee, 37205

Dear Mr. Huck:

We are in receipt of your letter offering your services as an Easter Egg psychic. There is a quarterly bulletin that we publish, but unfortunately the Spring edition comes out on April 10 - a few weeks past Easter. I guess there'll be a lot of missing eggs this year!

Thanks for thinking of us. We shall keep your information on file for future reference.

Sincerely,

Mary Rae
Consumer Services

MLR/dbb

April 11, 2002

Seattle Mariners
SAFECO Field
1250 1st Ave. S.
Seattle, WA 98134

Hello Seattle Mariners,

My name is Sterling Huck, but for years I've been known to baseball fans around the country as "The Roving Barber."

What do I do? I offer a fresh, close shave to men in the grandstands at ball games. My service begins with a piping hot towel, a facial massage, then a thick, creamy lather, applied with a special otter hair brush. My razor is sharpened weekly on a leather strop that hangs from my trousers. I pride myself on never cutting anyone, but just in case, I carry an array of styptic pencils. For rinsing, I carry a basin around my neck filled with water. It's quick, clean and easy. I've had many compliments from my customers that I provide the "best shave" they've ever had. And they can enjoy the ball game while I work. I even take care of maverick nose hairs and ingrown beards.

For years, I worked the minor club circuit with teams such as the Augusta Greenjackets, the Cancun Lobstermen and the Jupiter Hammerheads. I would love to offer my tonsorial skills exclusively to my favorite team, The Seattle Mariners! This year, I even have complimentary peppermint candies in the shape of tiny barber poles.

I'm looking forward to shaving the Seattle fans. Please let me know the details of how I apply for a license to shave.

Kind Regards,

Sterling Huck

Sterling Huck
3901 Whitland Ave. #27
Nashville, TN 37205

"Every shave is out of the park!"

"A Major League talent."

"Not a single error."

"My face feels baby smooth."

"He's no rookie."

"Go Mariners! Go Roving Barber!"

"He gave me candy."

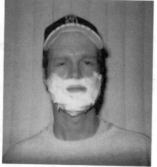

"He's the Sultan of the Strop."

"Lather me up!"

Seattle Mariners Fans Rave about the Roving Barber!!

Sterling Huck
3901 Whitland Ave. #27
Nashville, TN 37205

April 16, 2002

Dear Sterling,

Thank you for your interest in the Seattle Mariners. You have an amazingly unique
business. I will keep your information on file for future reference.

We wish you and your company the best of luck. Enjoy the 2002 baseball season.

Sincerely,

Cole Parsons
Promotions Coordinator
Seattle Mariners

November 5, 2001   **NO REPLY**

Farm Aid
11 Ward St.
Ste. 200
Somerville, MA 02143

Dear Farm Aid,

I admire the way you've helped the American farmer with ongoing benefit concerts. Our country was founded on the model of the agricultural man tilling the soil, planting crops, working sun-up until sundown, providing for us all. What a shame that the farmer is regularly trampled underfoot as we rush headlong into the information age. My old straw hat is off to Willie Nelson, Neil Young, John Cougar Mellencamp, Ted Nugent, Charlie Daniels and all the other fine performers for their fund-raising efforts.

I'm writing on behalf of another mutual friend of ours who is being regularly trampled underfoot. I'm talking about Formcidae Hymenopterous, more commonly known as the ant.

Did you know that every day in our country nearly 1.3 million ants meet an untimely end beneath the heels and soles of pedestrians? Many of these deaths are of course accidental, but many are deliberate. Undoubtedly, you've seen cruel children stamping anthills and torturing these innocent, industrious creatures. Tragic.

Two years ago, I started a group for the protection of our little segmented friends. Funding and support have been scarce, but I soldier on (I did get a nice check from Barbara Mandrell). I'm sure you've been in my position, maybe when you started Farm Aid. What I would like to propose is a collaboration between us, an offshoot event called "Ant Farm Aid."

"Ant Farm Aid" could be held on a satellite stage in the parking lot of the next Farm Aid. We could pass out educational pamphlets, show a documentary about how ants colonize and help the environment, and have some great live music to boot! Perhaps we could draw from the deep pool of talent you have at Farm Aid, and the artists could tailor their songs accordingly for my cause. For example, John Cougar Mellencamp could sing "A.N.T.S. in the U.S.A," Charlie Daniels could sing "The Ant's Gonna Do It Again" and Willie Nelson could sing, "Red Ants Crying In The Rain." Those are just a few suggestions. They could probably come up with more.

I really look forward to working with you on "Ant Farm Aid." Please reply soon.

Best Regards,

Sterling Huck

Sterling Huck
3901 Whitland Ave. #27
Nashville, TN 37205

October 10, 2001

St. Louis Zoo
Forest Park
St. Louis, MO 63139

Hello St. Louis Zoo,

I have my own business, called Venison Jerky On Wheels. As the name suggests, I sell venison jerky from the back of a truck. It's a bright red vehicle with a cartoon of a buck lying in a hammock painted on the side, with fiberglass antlers mounted on the front cab.

I've been traveling around the country for years. Everyone loves my venison jerky, which I cure and smoke myself. I once sold a pound of the jerky to the actor Robert Urich. He told me it was the best he'd ever had, and if I was near his house, he'd buy my venison jerky every other day.

I have plenty of wet-naps for easy clean-up.

I'd like to get permission to park my Venison Jerky On Wheels business outside the St. Louis Zoo during the week of November 12-19.

Thanks for your kind consideration. I can give two-for-one jerky discounts to zoo employees. No problemo.

Best Regards,

Sterling Huck
3901 Whitland Ave. #27
Nashville, TN 37205

P.S. - Do you have peccaries?

SAINT LOUIS ZOO

One   Government   Drive   •   Saint   Louis,   MO   63110

October 12, 2001

Mr. Sterling Huck
3901 Whitland Ave. #27
Nashville, TN 37205

Dear Mr. Huck:

While I personally enjoy jerky, and your venison jerky sounds great, it would not be possible for you to park your Venison Jerky on Wheels outside of the Saint Louis Zoo. Such vendors are prohibited by law in Forest Park where the Zoo is located.

All revenue producing activities within the Zoo are operated by the Zoo with the total revenue produced going toward the Zoo's operation, the care of the animals and our conservation programs. The Zoo is part of a subdistrict of the State of Missouri.

By the way, we have chacoan peccaries on display in the antelope area. You certainly are welcome to visit them.

Sincerely,

Charles H. Hoessle
Director

NO REPLY

June 14, 2001

Pottery Barn
3250 Van Ness Ave.
San Francisco, CA 94109

Dear Pottery Barn,

I'm planning to open a chain of seven stores in the Southeast, called Poverty Barn.

We will sell "found art" pieces from low-income neighborhoods and third world countries. Our merchandise will have a rough-hewn charm and unflinching integrity that I believe will appeal to people from all economic backgrounds. Some examples of what we'll be offering:

Plastic milk jug "piggy banks"
Mr. Pibb wind chimes
Baby doll parts
Uruguayan piñata full of salad
Bangladesh midget walking sticks

I realize that the name Poverty Barn is similar to Pottery Barn, but we will offset this by using an all lower-case logo in bright pink.

Our flagship store will open this October in Biloxi, Mississippi.

Regards,

Sterling Huck
3901 Whitland Ave. #27
Nashville, TN 37205

February 12, 1999

Dr. Henry Kissinger
435 E. 52 St.
New York, NY 10022

NO REPLY

Dear Dr. Kissinger,

Warm greetings to you! My name is Sterling Huck. In the southern U.S., I am fast gaining a reputation for my unparalleled ability in that ultimate match of concentration and control - the staring contest. What started as a local pursuit has blossomed into a full-time career, as I've challenged and beaten celebrity opponents such as Andre Agassi, Lee Majors, Elvira and William Lee Golden of The Oak Ridge Boys.

I'm writing to you not only because of your political accomplishments but because you are a man with a fierce, intense gaze. A most worthy opponent, I believe. I'd like to challenge you to a staring contest. The first one who glances away or laughs, speaks or breaks a straight face, loses.

As I realize you have many commitments, I ask you to name the most convenient date, time and place for our staring contest, and I will be there. If it's okay, the documentary maker Indigo Matahi would like to film the two of us engaged in the staring contest.

You may be interested to know that I am also currently developing a book on the subject, entitled *The Art Of Staring*.

Thank you for your consideration and I look forward to matching gazes with you soon.

Best Regards,

Sterling Huck
3901 Whitland Ave. #27
Nashville, TN 37205

P.S. - You can remove your glasses or wear them for the contest. Whatever you wish.

November 18, 1997

U.S. Marine Corps
Headquarters
Washington, DC 20380

Dear Gentlemen,

I was delighted to hear about your new branch of the armed services, the "Weekend Marines." As someone who's always dreamt of a life in the military, but has never had the time, this seems like the perfect solution. Now I can keep my job as assistant manager of the Orange Julius and every Friday trade in my foam rubber shirt and paper hat for some dress blues and a smart white cap.

I'm writing to find out more about the program. What kinds of drills and maneuvers will be involved? Does a "Weekend Marine" get regular issue uniforms and weapons? Does he get to visit different bases and forts? Are there simulated combat games and recreations of famous battles? Is there an opportunity for advancement of rank (ie, "Weekend Lieutenants" and "Weekend Five Star Generals")?

Please send me information regarding this exciting new branch of the military. I'm ready to report for duty as a "Weekend Marine."

Best Regards,

Sterling Huck
3901 Whitland Ave. #27
Nashville, TN 37205

P.S. - I have a canteen.

Marines

PHONE·A·GRAM.

I HAVE NOT BEEN ABLE TO REACH YOU BY PHONE.
I'D LIKE TO GET TOGETHER WITH YOU AND TALK
ABOUT THE CHALLENGES THE MARINE CORPS
HAS TO OFFER. CHALLENGES THAT DEVELOP YOUR
MIND AS WELL AS YOUR BODY. PLEASE CALL
ME AT _298-1407_ OR I WILL BE BY AFTER
JAN 15, 1998 TO SEE YOU AND YOUR FAMILY.

Marine Recruiter

Marines

HONOR.   COURAGE.   COMMITMENT.

James P. Norman Jr.
Staff Sergeant
U.S. Marine Corps

Marine Corps Recruiting
731 Thompson Lane
Suite 103
Nashville, TN 37204
(615) 298-1407/9929/9976
Fax: (615) 386-3370

March 5, 1998

Quaker Oats Co.
P.O. Box 049001
Chicago, IL 60604-9001
Attn: King Vitaman

To Quaker Oats,

I've been a fan of King Vitaman cereal for many years. In fact, hardly a morning goes by when I'm not lapping up the scrumptious, fortified crunchy nuggets bathed in milk. I'm happy to be one of the King's royal subjects!

But lately, as I've studied the cereal box, I've noticed that King Vitaman is looking older and somehow sadder. He's smiling, but it's a strained, joyless smile. At first I thought this was my imagination, but I've saved nearly every empty box of King Vitaman cereal I've eaten for the last three years. When I compared pictures of the King from 1995 to late 1997, the change was startling. From happy to sad.

The aging process is natural, of course, but I wonder if the King's melancholia is due to something else, such as a lack of a suitable heir to his crunchy cereal throne. As a lover of breakfast and an actor (I recently played a police officer in the independent film *Tall, Dark & Handcuffed*), I'd like to offer my services as a possible successor when and if King Vitaman abdicates or passes on. Perhaps I could be known as Prince Nutrient. At first, the King and I could appear together on the cereal box to familiarize your breakfast patrons with my face. Then eventually, the scepter could pass and I would be known as King Vitaman II.

I've attached a photo so you can get an idea of how I'd look as the new royal spokesman for your cereal. I'm wearing a stage prop crown, which isn't quite as regal-looking as King Vitaman's deluxe model.

Please let me know when I can begin my training. And tell his royal majesty I'm a big, big fan.

Yours Sincerely,

Sterling Huck (The Man Who Would Be King Vitaman II)
3901 Whitland Ave. #27
Nashville, TN 37205

Dodging the issue of whether or not there was unrest in the court of King Vitaman, Quaker Oats refused to pass the royal scepter to Sterling Huck.

April 15, 2002

Wild West Weekend
c/o City Hall
214 C Street
Washington, KS 66968

Dear Wild West Weekend,

I am the former blacksmith of colonial Williamsburg, VA. For ten years, I forged the steel, smelted the iron and stuck my poker into the red hot fire. I made customized horseshoes and thimbles. I talked to the visitors about the lost art of blacksmithery, and had my picture taken with folks of all ages. It was a wonderful life, and now it is no more.

Currently, I am staying with a friend in Nashville, TN, trying to get my bearings, doing the odd "smithing" job here and there. I've repaired a backstop and a catcher's mask for the Nashville Sounds ball team. I've also fitted some local fillies.

I would like to be part of your Wild West Weekend this August. Please let me know the requirements. I could send some of my work, if you prefer, perhaps an engraved horseshoe, or a head bust I made of the comedian Buddy Hackett out of iron ore.

Thanks for your consideration. I look forward to hearing from you. I'm traveling by horse, so I could probably arrive in two weeks time.

Kindest Regards,

Sterling Huck, Blacksmith
3901 Whitland Ave. #27
Nashville, TN 37205

214 C Street
County Courthouse
Washington, KS 66968

April 18, 2002

Sterling Huck
3901 Whitland Ave. #27
Nashville, TN 37205

Sterling,

We would love to have you this August! The Pony Express Festival is Sunday, August 25, from 9:00 to 4:00. We will have an appreciation dinner the night before for those of you that travel to the event. There is no cost to come and demonstrate. We play a pony express reride, chuckwagon, musical entertainment, civil war reenactment, fast-draw contest, bar-b-q lunch, quilt raffle and much more. If you would send me your mailing address, I will send you a registration form and meal ticket, etc. I look forward to hearing from you.

As the Economic Development Director of Washington County, it would not be right for me to let you go without saying that if you are looking for a business opportunity, we could sure put you to work here in Washington. We have some available business space and there is a big need for welders and metal workers. Let me know if you are interested in starting a business, I will bet you would love it here!

Sincerely,

Karen Latta

April 17, 2002

Mayor Carolyn Risher
135 Highway 40 W
Inglis, FL 34449

Dear Mayor Risher,

I would like to bring my business, Handtowels Of Turin, to Inglis. In light of the recent banning of the Devil in your town, I think the time is right.

A little about me. I'm a Christian. I work out of a converted winnebago. My assistant Argo keeps tabs on the money.

Each of my handtowels is 100% cotton, 12" x 18", and stained with a mysterious shrouded image that may or may not be the face of Jesus. These towels can be lucky totems or simply conversation piece-type souvenirs. They're versatile. Even if you're skeptical about the controversial religious image, they're still handsome towels, and they will absorb perspiration. Everyone is a winner!

I would like to sell the Handtowels Of Turin to the tourists in Inglis this summer. Please send me the necessary documents.

Kind Regards,

Sterling Huck
3901 Whitland Ave. #27
Nashville, TN 37205
USA

February 6, 2002

Carolyn Risher
P.O. Drawer 429
Inglis, Fl. 34449-0429

Dear *Friend*,

First of all I want to apologize for taking so long to answer your wonderful letters and cards of comfort and support.

You will never know how uplifting your words of encouragement meant to me. I believe if I had not received your cards and letters assuring me that you were lifting me up in your prayers, I would not have been able to stand strong and firm as God has surely kept me in his loving care and protection.

We as children of God have got to bind together, pray for each other and let the world know that we are not ashamed to stand in the face of evil and tell the world we are the chosen ones.

Evil has been rampant way too long. Our generation has gone slack, carefree, cold and unable to face the difficulties of life. They are not willing to turn to the Almighty God and repent for their sins and come to know God as their redeemer and protector.

I thank God every day that I have a family out there that prays for me. I hope one day I will be able to meet each and every one of you in person so I can show just how grateful and appreciative I am for all your love and prayers. I want to let you know that you are also in my prayers to God for you and your family.

Please continue to pray for me. I look forward to hearing from you and most of all I look forward to meeting you.

Your Sister in Christ,

Carolyn Risher

Carolyn Risher

P.S. Call town hall, they will talk to you about your business
352 447-2203

135 Highway 40 West
Post Office Drawer 429
Inglis, Florida 34449

PROCLAMATION

Be it known from this day forward that Satan, ruler of darkness, giver of evil, destroyer of what is good and just, is not now, nor ever again will be, a part of this town of Inglis. Satan is hereby declared powerless, no longer ruling over, nor influencing, our citizens.

In the past, Satan has caused division, animosity, hate, confusion, ungodly acts on our youth, and discord amoung our friends and loved ones. NO LONGER!

The body of Jesus Christ, those citizens cleansed by the Blood of the Lamb, hereby join together to bind the forces of evil in the Holy Name of Jesus. We have taken our town back for the Kingdom of God. We are taking everything back that the devil ever stole from us. We will never again be deceived by satanic and demonic forces.

As blood-bought children of God, we exercise our authority over the devil in Jesus' name. By that authority, and through His Blessed Name, we command all satanic and demonic forces to cease their activities and depart the town of Inglis.

As the Mayor of Inglis, duly elected by the citizens of this town, and appointed by God to this position of leadership, I proclaim victory over Satan, freedom for our citizens, and liberty to worship our Creator and Heavenly Father, the God of Israel. I take this action in accordance with the words of our Lord and Savior, Jesus Christ, as recorded in Matthew 28:18-20 and Mark 16:15-18.

Signed and seal this 5th day of November, 2001.

CAROLYN RISHER, MAYOR

SALLY McCRANIE, TOWN CLERK

May 25, 1998

NO REPLY

King Hassan II
Royal Palace
Rabat, Morocco

Dear King Hassan II,

I know you're a busy man so I'll get right to the point. I'd like to apply for the job of court jester to Your Royal Highness.

I feel I am qualified for this job in many ways. I can play the lute, sing funny songs, tell ribald stories, pose riddles, make suggestive and rude sounds with my mouth. I can turn somersaults and run very fast. I can compose short poems on the spot for any occasion. Suppose it was your birthday. I might say (and I'm just improvising here):

Old King Hassan bids farewell
to another year, though you can't tell.
He looks so trim and sleek and vital
and that's fitting for his royal title . . .

Of course, I'd learn to say it in your native tongue of Tamazight. If I'm hired I could bring along a full court jester costume including pointy shoes and a jingling hat. And I have a trunk full of props - magic wands, pirate teeth, plastic fat stomachs, clown noses, dribble glasses, slide whistles, rubber vomit and much more. I would keep you entertained every minute of the day. I'm always in a happy mood. With all the problems you have in the middle East, I could offer the perfect antidote - laughs and sunny times and games and more!

So please tell me how to arrange an audition so I can show you some of my stunts and tricks. I will be your best court jester!

With Laughter,

Sterling Huck

Sterling Huck
3901 Whitland Ave. #27
Nashville, TN 37205

February 27, 1998

Cozymel's Restaurant
c/o Brinker Int'l.
6820 LBJ Freeway
Dallas, TX 75240

Dear Cozymel's,

I'm currently in financial negotiations to open a nightclub called "Cozy Mel's Place" in Brentwood, TN. The theme of my club is based on Chicago, circa 1920's. There will be hot jazz music, dancing, liquor and a decor that pays loving tribute to the time with old newspaper clippings, photographs and signs, as well as mementos like lapel carnations and carbine machine guns (not real ones, of course). I'm naming the club in honor of my late great-grandfather, Charles Melvin Huck, who was a well-known character in the Chicago of the 20s. His nickname was "Cozy Mel." Apparently, he had a way with the ladies!

I realize of course that the name, "Cozy Mel's Place," is slightly reminiscent of your restaurant, "Cozymel's," though the pronunciation (not to mention the atmosphere) is completely different. The "o" in my "Cozy" is a long sound, like "ROSIE greer" or "panty HOSE," while yours rhymes, if I'm not mistaken, with "GAUZE" or "crazy STRAWS." Also, there is a space between the "y" and the "M." Two words: "Cozy Mel's." Then the "Place" makes it totally different.

The planned location of my club is far enough away - about 3.5 miles from the Cozymel's in Brentwood - that it shouldn't be a problem for either of us, or for our customers. In fact, we may be able to work together to promote each other's businesses, giving away 2-for-1 coupons and paper hats and so forth.

I thought I'd write to make you aware of my plans to open "Cozy Mel's Place" this August. Please let your employees know, so when patrons start enquiring about "Cozy Mel's," they'll know where to send them. Thank you.

Best Regards,

Sterling Huck

Sterling Huck
3901 Whitland Ave. #27
Nashville, TN 37205

Cozymel's served up a generous helping of steaming hot legalese that left Sterling with a slightly bloated feeling. After considering a few other alternate names—Coyote Mel's, Snug & Cozy's Place, John Cougar Mel's—he decided the restaurant business wasn't for him.

September 21, 1998

Avis Rent-A-Car
900 Old Country Road
Garden City, NY 11530

Dear Avis,

My job as a photographer of nature in the wild keeps me on the go constantly, and you'll be glad to hear that Avis has always been right there with me! Of all the car rental companies I've tried, Avis is the best. For service, friendliness and reliability, I'd give the trophy to the "Big A."

Since you've always been able to accommodate me in the past, I'm hoping you'll be able to fill a rather special request. I've been given an assignment by National Geographic this coming December to photograph the rare and beautiful midget polar bears on Ostrova Vrangelya, an island in the Arctic Ocean.

I'd like to take an Avis Rent-A-Car with me. I will be accompanied on this trip by former football pro Dick Butkus. If Dick and I can pick up the car somewhere in Alaska, then we can have a ferry take us across the Bering Strait to our final destination. We'd need the car for three weeks and we'd like it to be equipped with snow tires (perhaps even chains), lots of anti-freeze, a reliable heater and a good ice scraper (not the handheld kind).

There aren't many cars in Ostrova Vrangelya, so aside from the occasional slippery patch in the road, I don't think we'll have any traffic problems. There may be some angry fur trappers about, but in their cumbersome clothes, they'll never be able to keep up with us.

If you'd like I could photograph some of the midget polar bears playing near or on the Avis Rent-A-Car. It might make a cute, effective photo for an ad. Maybe Dick Butkus could get in the shot too.

Please let me know if I can rely on Avis for this exciting assignment.

Best Regards,

Sterling Huck
3901 Whitland Ave. #27
Nashville, TN 37205

AVIS.
We try harder.®

Avis Rent A Car
System, Inc.

WORLD WIDE RESERVATION
CENTER
4500 South 129th East Avenue
P.O. Box 699000
Tulsa, Oklahoma 74169-9000

Telephone: (800) 352-7900

October 20, 1998

Mr. Sterling Huck
3901 Whitland Ave. #27
Nashville, Tennessee   37205

Dear Mr. Huck,

Thank you for contacting Avis. Your trip sounds like an exciting one.

The Avis operation in Alaska is a franchise operation. They have been provided with a copy of your letter to determine if they can accommodate your car rental request. Unfortunately they cannot provide you with what you will need.

They are suggesting that you will need to get your vehicle in Nome. The Avis Franchise does not serve Nome, Alaska. There are two car rental companies in Nome. You may want to contact them to determine if either can provide you with what you need.

Stampede Rent A Car   907-443-3838

Alaska Cabs   907-443-2939

Thank you for your business.

January 9, 1996

The Coca-Cola Company
Consumer Affairs Dept.
Atlanta, GA 30301

Dear Friends,

I've been enjoying your soft drink ever since I was knee high to a cicada. In fact, my friends and family often joke that I must've been weened on Coca-Cola instead of mother's milk. I don't know about that, but I do love "The Real Thing."

I'm writing to inform you that on a yet-to-be-determined day this spring, I will be shooting for a world's record in Coca-Cola drinking. The most I've ever had in one 24-hour period is thirty-one 12-oz. cans. But I will go far, far beyond that. I will drink 30 gallons of Coca-Cola in one day.

A local farmer named Fred Backer has agreed to donate troughs that he uses to feed his animals. The Coca-Cola will be poured into the troughs by a panel of impartial judges and I will drink it. I've written to the Guiness Book people in hopes of getting them to fly over for this event. Perhaps you want to send a Coca-Cola agent too.

I'll be in touch when all the particulars are set.

Coke is it!

Best Regards,

Sterling Huck
3901 Whitland Ave. #27
Nashville, TN 37205

The Coca-Cola Company

COCA-COLA PLAZA
ATLANTA, GEORGIA

ADDRESS REPLY TO
P. O. DRAWER 1734
ATLANTA, GA 30301

1-800-438-2653

January 22, 1996

Mr. Sterling Huck
3901 Whitland Ave., No. 27
Nashville, TN 37205

Dear Sterling:

Thank you for your recent letter. We were delighted to hear from you.

Sterling, you are an ambitious young man! Unfortunately, I am unable to
provide you with the name of the person who has consumed the most Coca-Cola in
a 24-hour period. I can, however, share with you an amazing statistic. Did
you know that if all the Coca-Cola ever produced was packaged in 6-1/2 ounce
bottles and these were placed end to end, they would wrap around the equator
21,161 times? I have enclosed a couple of brochures full of fun facts about
our Company I hope you will enjoy.

We do wish you much success in your goal. It is consumers like you who keep
us on top year after year! If you have any questions about the materials,
please feel free to give us a call here at 1-800-438-2653. Best wishes!

Sincerely,

Kimberly D. Russell
Kimberly D. Russell
Consumer Affairs Specialist

Encl: Facts, Figures and Features
        Olympic Torch Relay Map
        Polar Bear Poster - under separate cover
        Sticker Postcard
        Refreshing Facts

April 10, 2002

City of Andalusia
P.O. Box 429
Andalusia, AL 36420

Dear Andalusia,

In Flannadu did Sterling Huck a stately new superstore decree!

Yes, I would like to bring a new business to your town. And as you may have guessed, it's called Flannadu. It will be a flan lover's paradise, a superstore more super than any superstore! 101 varieties of flan and spongecake, with fillings galore - raspberry, blueberry, apple, strawberry, banana, cherry, grape, scrod, you name it!

In keeping with the theme of Coleridge's classic poem, the employees of Flannadu will be dressed like ancient barbaric warriors - the uniform includes animal pelts, bone clubs, domed helmets, furry boots and a special barbarian scent called "Khan For The Day" (the scent will also be for sale at Flannadu). While the employees may look fearsome, they will be friendly to the customers, and knowledgeable about flan.

Please send me the necessary forms and let me know a suitable location for Flannadu! The famous actor Harry Dean Stanton has agreed to appear at the opening.

Sincerely,

Sterling Huck
3901 Whitland Ave. #27
Nashville, TN 37205

P.S. - Andalusia = Flandalusia.

THE CITY OF

Andalusia

EARL V. JOHNSON, Mayor
PAM STEELE, City Clerk
THOMAS B. ALBRITTON, City Attorney
PATRICK S. McCALMAN, Judge

P.O. BOX 429
ANDALUSIA, ALABAMA 36420
TELEPHONE (334) 222-3311 • 222-3312 • 222-3313
FAX (334) 222-5114

CITY COUNCIL
Bridges D. Anderson
Michael L. Jones, Jr.
Andy Alexander
Jerry B. Andrews
Harry R. Hinson

April 19, 2002

Mr. Sterling Huck
3901 Whitland Avenue #27
Nashville, Tennessee 37205

Dear Mr. Huck:

Fe Fi Fo Fum, we smell the blood of Prankster Scum!!! We were flabbergasted to receive your flamboyant letter about flan; however, Andalusia has been declared a "Flan Free Zone." We don't like flan because flan flops in Andalusia; in other words, flan don't float.

We don't like flans, flags, fleas, fleflikers, floats, flaws, flannel, flares, flat-heads, flat-tops, floaters, floggers, flubs (bunglers and botchers), flies, flippers, flab, flunkies, flutes, floozies (discount this one), flim-flammers, flakes (frosted or otherwise). We don't even like women named Flo, so take your flan and GO!

Sincerely,

Earl V. Johnson,
Mayor of Andalusia
"Committed to a Flan Free Society"

P.S. Flaunting flannery in Andalusia is not permitted, but flan floats in Florala.

A Certified City • Prepared For Industry

June 15, 2002

Wizard Of Oz Festival
Duneland Chamber Of Commerce
220 W. Broadway
Chesterton, IN 46304

Hello Fellow Oz Lovers!

I was so very excited to read about your annual festival that pays tribute
to the greatest movie musical of all time, *The Wizard Of Oz*.

It sounds like you have a wonderful program planned, what with the
costumed characters and original Munchkins (they must be getting on in
years if they're original!). If there is room on the yellow brick road, I would
like to offer my services.

For years, I have been perfecting my stage act: Margaret Hamilton as The
Wicked Witch Of The West. Unlike other drag performers who gravitate to
the glitzy and the glamorous - Cher, Dolly Parton, Barbra Streisand - I
chose to become the wonderful actress Margaret Hamilton, and it's been
the most fulfilling role of my life! With my wig, black dress, pointy hat,
green make-up and nose wart, I look in the mirror and say, "Hello, my
pretty!" then cackle loudly. I have even trained three spider monkeys to
accompany me on stage as my servants and foot soldiers. Sadly, they
cannot fly, but they do have acrobatic talents.

In my forty-minute set, I pedal a stationary bicycle like mad (as Miss
Gulch). I rub my hands with glee. I look into a crystal ball. I fly across the
stage on a broom (with the help of a wire system). And for my finale, I
"melt" into the floor, leaving only my hat and a mass of steaming goo. It's
spectacular. Then afterwards, I return as Aunt Cora, the older Maxwell
House coffee-era Margaret, for a Q & A with the audience.

It is the ultimate Oz-related act, and I believe it would be a perfect fit for
your Wizard Of Oz Festival this September!

Please let me know if I can jumpstart my broom and fly on over.

Surrender Dorothy!

Sterling Huck (is . . . Margaret Hamilton)
3901 Whitland Ave. #27
Nashville, TN 37205

21st Annual Wizard of Oz Festival
September 20th, 21st, 22nd 2002

Sponsored by

The Duneland Chamber of Commerce
220 Broadway
Chesterton, IN 46304

Phone
(219) 926-5513

Fax
(219) 926-7395

E-mail
dunelandchamber@niia.net

2002 Chairperson
Barb Pinks

Co-Chairperson
Laurie
Franke-Polz

June 24, 2002

Sterling Huck
3901 Whitland Avenue
27
Nashville, TN 37205

Dear Sterling (aka Margaret Hamilton)

Thank you for your recent letter dated June 15, 2002. Your Margaret Hamilton impersonation sounds fantastic, but I'm afraid our Wicked Witch of the West would get her green warty nose out of joint if we brought in another Witch.

We commission actors and actresses to perform as our official costume characters for the weekend. Many of our cast has been with us since the inception of the festival 21 years ago. Therefore, I will have to reluctantly decline your generous offer.

I hope however you will visit this year's festival and join in the fun with us!! I have enclosed a preliminary event guide for your review.

Sincerely,

Laurie J. Franke-Polz
Executive Director

NO REPLY

April 10, 2000

Corvallis City Manager
420 NW Second Street
Corvallis, OR 97330

Dear Corvallis,

I am writing to inquire about a permit to open a new business in your town. It is called "Ma & Pa's House Of Trephining."

Many ancient tribal cultures believed that illness and unhappiness could be cured by releasing evil spirits trapped inside a person's head. The lost art of trephining - or trepanning, as it is sometimes erroneously called - is the answer.

By drilling tiny holes in the skull of a patient, we can produce immediate effects and begin the healing process. We have treated everything from back pain to diabetes to manic depression. And the good news is that trephining is relatively painless. Both my wife and I - we call ourselves "Ma & Pa" for a folksy, homespun touch - are trained in this lost art, having studied with shamen and tribal doctors throughout South America and East Asia.

I am also the curator of The Spatula Museum in Kermitville, KS, as well as a partner in Incendiary, Inc., a company that specializes in home flamethrowers, so I already have a track record of success.

We would like to test market "Ma & Pa's House Of Trephining" for a year in Corvallis.

Please let me know the details for setting up our business in your town. Thank you very much.

Best Regards,

Sterling Huck
3901 Whitland Ave. #27
Nashville, TN 37205

The Creative Impulse

September 12, 1995

Six Flags Over Texas
P.O. Box 90191
Arlington, TX 76004

Dear Six Flags,

I'm an independent film maker, currently working on a humorous short called
Leash-ure Time, in which dogs are seen enjoying various human leisure
activities. For example, I've filmed two Miniature Schnauzers at a bowling alley,
a Springer Spaniel at a tanning salon and a Whippet watching a movie at a
theater.

The reason I'm writing is to request permission to shoot some footage for
Leash-ure Time at your park - specifically on the Texas Giant rollercoaster. My
idea is to have five Chihuahuas riding the Giant. Of course, I'd adhere to all
safety standards of your park, but as these are all well-behaved dogs (they're
mine) that will sit still and stay unless told otherwise, I don't foresee any
problems (most dogs can withstand a G-Force of up to +4.25). You may want to
suggest additional means of securing the dogs in the rollercoaster carriages.

The whole shoot would only take a few minutes - the span of a rollercoaster
ride - and I would be more than willing to pay whatever you deem your losses
would be for the customers who'd be pre-empted from riding at that particular
time.

Your park will be portrayed in the best possible light, and the audience will be
made to understand that you don't actually admit Chihuahuas or any kind of
dogs as paying customers.

Thanks so much for your consideration. I look forward to hearing from you.

Kind Regards,

Sterling Huck
3901 Whitland Ave. #27
Nashville, TN 37205

Six Flags
Over Texas
A TIME WARNER ENTERTAINMENT COMPANY

September 22, 1995

Mr. Sterling Huck
3901 Whitland Ave. #27
Nashville, TN 37205

Mr. Huck,

Thanks so much for thinking to include us in your film project, "Leash-ure Time." It sounds like a fun project!

Unfortunately, we will not be able to participate in the film. Despite your dog's good behavior, it simply would not be safe for your dogs to ride the Texas Giant. I have to say, we've had some unusual requests over the years for the Giant - but yours is definitely the best yet.

The visual of your idea sounds very fun and entertaining, but we cannot participate. I hope you understand. Thank you for writing us - we do appreciate you thinking of Six Flags Over Texas.

We wish you the best of luck with your film and future projects.

Sincerely,

Nancy St. Pierre
Public Relations Manager

March 19, 2002

Reg Whitworth, Development Officer of Belper
c/o Tourist Information Centre
Town Hall, Market Place, Ripley
Derbyshire DE5 3BT, England

Dear Mr. Whitworth,

Outrage. That's what I felt this morning when I read the news item about children attacking the giant Mr. Potato Head on display in your town. The spud ambassador of goodwill deserves respect and kindness, not scratching and torn limbs. Sadly, I think this vandalism is symptomatic of our times.

I know you're at a loss about what to do with Mr. Potato Head. I may be able to help. I'm one of America's foremost sculptors of roadside statuary. Gorillas, polar bears, giant robots - that sort of thing. I have an idea. What if Mr. Potato Head had two bodyguards? Meet Mr. P and Hong Kong Potato!

Mr. P, modeled after the world's most famous bodyguard, Mr. T, would be a potato with a mohawk ridge and an attitude. I could equip him with a voicebox that said, "I pity the fool who tries to hurt Mr. Potato Head!" and "You want a piece of Mr. PH, you gotta deal with Mr. P first!" I could also add a heating element which would make Mr. P's skin over 480 degrees Fahrenheit - as hot as a baked potato just out of the oven. That would make vandals think twice.

His partner, Hong Kong Potato, would have limbs that kicked and chopped with ferocious accuracy. Perhaps I could figure out a way to give him that Crouching Tiger, Floating Dragon-like ability to defy gravity and deliver his deadly blows to trespassers from mid-air.

I've included rough sketches of the two bodyguards for your inspection. Please let me know if you're interested and we can talk specifics.

I'm sorry about what happened to Mr. Potato Head. Here's hoping we can protect him in the future!

Best Regards,

Sterling Huck

Sterling Huck
3901 Whitland Ave. #27
Nashville, TN 37205

"Mr. P"

"Hong Kong Potato"

Sterling Huck
3901 Whitland Ave. #27
Nashville
TN 37205
USA

23 April 2002

Dear Mr Huck:

I was pleased to receive your letter of 19 March 2002 and subsequent e-mail of 19 April 2001 regarding Mr Potato Head. Unfortunately, we have the disadvantage of not seeing the press about this particular sculpture although I am aware that the stories have generated interest Worldwide.

The truth of the matter is that Mr Potato Head has been standing in public places in Towns in this area since the end of May last year and on only one occasion has he suffered any deliberate damage, and even that is arguable because he was damaged when a group of people were trying to put him onto the top of a flat-roofed building to give him a better profile. The scratching which has occurred is from being constantly loaded onto trucks to take him from place to place. The ideal way of transportation is to stand him flat onto a pick-up truck but we have not always had access to that type of vehicle.

Mr Potato Head has been standing outside a superstore since 6 March 2002 without any problem and will soon be moved to a charity event at a hotel. He is a Superstar who costs a lot less than Stallone or Schwarzeneggar!

I am grateful for your kind offer to provide further sculptures to act as bodyguards and there are two important issues to be considered. Firstly, there may be Copyright issues for the use of images which undoubtedly demand fees. Secondly, I expect the cost of producing the figures to be high, as would be the transportation costs.

Your further comments will be appreciated.

Yours sincerely

Reg Whitworth
Tourism Development Officer

Tourism Unit

Town Hall Ripley
Derbyshire East Midlands DE5 3BT
Tel: 01773 570222 Fax: 01773 841487
Minicom: 01773 841490
E-Mail: enquiry@ambervalley.gov.uk
Web: www.ambervalley.gov.uk

Caring and Working for Amber Valley

March 4, 2002

Burns Rodeo
P.O. Box 2100
Burns, KS 67021

Dear Burns Rodeo,

I am a rodeo clown who dresses like Johann Sebastian Bach. I wear a plush vermilion velvet coat, tight at the waist and flared at the hips, a frilly shirt with ruffled sleeves and of course a magnificent powdered high-pile wig, tied in back with a catogan. To all appearances, I am J.S. Bach. The only difference is I do tricks with livestock.

And I do it to an all-Bach soundtrack. Imagine me lassoing a maniac bull to the sounds of "Minuet In G." Or riding a bronc while the Brandenburg Concerto provides a lively counterpoint. And then I'll tie up a hog to "Bouree."

I'd love to perform my show, "Bach In The Saddle," at your rodeo! I'd only need airfare and modest lodgings. I'll find the horses and bulls once I'm there.

After my performance, I sell souvenir teat rings.

Please let me know as soon as possible about the arrangements for my "Bach In The Saddle" show at the Burns Rodeo this summer. I'm ready to rope and ride!

Yours Truly,

Sterling Huck
3901 Whitland Ave. #27
Nashville, TN 37205

BURNS RODEO

ESTABLISHED 1957, BURNS, KS

March 11, 2002

Sterling Huck
#27
3901 Whitland Ave.
Nashville, TN 37205

Hello Sterling,

Thank you for your interest in the Burns Rodeo. Your show sounds entertaining; however, rodeo performances have already been scheduled for this year by our rodeo committee.

We'll keep you on file for next year. Best of luck.

Sincerely,

Ned Mayfield

Ned Mayfield
Coordinator, Burns Rodeo

April 16, 2002

Johnny Counterfit
Singing Impressionist
P.O. Box 292767
Nashville, TN 37205

Dear Johnny Counterfit,

I enjoyed your website. Your impressions are terrific, especially your Johnny Cash!

I wanted to tell you that my parakeet José Ferrer is an aspiring impressionist!

José is something of a feathered prodigy, I believe, blessed with the audio equivalent (for birds) of photographic memory. His powers of mimicry are so great that he can imitate all the members of my family, our appliances, the telephone, the front door closing, the wind, the rain, even celebrities on TV. He does a Regis Philbin that you wouldn't believe.

I would like to put José on the stage, doing an act, but I don't want to confuse or frighten him. What are your feelings about bird acts? Do you know of any talent agents that specialize in birds? Would you ever consider having a parakeet open a show for you?

Thanks for starting José on the road to what may be fame and fortune. I look forward to your expert advice.

Kind Regards,

Sterling Huck
3901 Whitland Ave. #27
Nashville, TN 37205

The Johnny Counterfit® Show
Comedian/Singing Impressionist
J.C. Productions & Entertainment Corp.
P.O. Box 292767 Nashville, TN 37229
Tel: 615.885.9500 E-Mail: JCVoices@aol.com Web: www.johnnycounterfit.com

Hi Huck:

Although many consider we impressionists "bird brained," I have never given it a second thought, a "fowl" derogatory remark though it is. My suggestion would be to start by booking "Jose" in state and county fairs, as well as television and radio programs; perhaps Jay Leno and/or David Letterman would be interested in your feathered friend.

Try any number of booking agents in your local area who may have national/international connections, but be careful they don't brand you a "Huck-ster."

As for using "Jose" on my show, It wouldn't be a good idea to give my audience "the bird."

Good Luck,
Johnny Counterfit

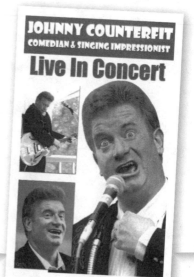

June 15, 1997

National Fluid Milk Processor Promotion Board
1250 H St. NW
Ste. 900
Washington, DC 20005

Dear Sirs,

I've enjoyed your colorful ads featuring various celebrities sporting milk mustaches. I too am a milk lover and a big believer in the importance of calcium in our daily diets. While I'm not a star of the caliber of Lisa Kudrow, Tony Bennett or Lee Majors, I do possess a rare talent which I believe may interest you.

For the past 23 years, I've worked with various circuses and touring troupes under the stage name "Sgt. Milko." Part of my act consists of drinking a full glass of milk and leaving not only a milk mustache, but also a milk goatee and milk sideburns. It involves some creative dribbling and quick head maneuvers! I have mastered it to the point where I can actually attain various styles: for example, Milk Muttonchops (like Elvis), Milk Man Chu (an oriental look) and Ulysses S. Milk (a full dripping beard) - these are just a few of the milk disguises I've used to delight audiences from 3 to 93.

I'd like to offer my services to your promotion board for a future magazine ad, or perhaps as a creative consultant.

Thanks for your interest and I look forward to working with you.

Sincerely,

Sterling Huck ("Sgt. Milko")
3901 Whitland Ave. #27
Nashville, TN 37205

**Although impressed with
Sgt. Milko's obvious abilities,
MilkPEP decided to stick with more
recognizable faces for their ads.**

August 26, 1996

Cincinnati Art Museum
Eden Park
Cincinnati, OH 45202-1596

Dear CAM,

I understand that you have an outstanding collection of art related to the Old
West. This has been a special interest of mine for many years. In fact, I have
two rooms in my house dedicated to nothing but Old West-style art (much to the
chagrin of my lady). My favorite works to collect are portraits of Hollywood
legend John Wayne, and I have amassed over one hundred and thirty, from
small charcoal sketches to laminated wood clocks to my prized possession, a
spectacular 8-ft. tall sculpture of the *True Grit*-era Duke, made completely from
Play-Doh. It's something to behold. I wish John Wayne was alive so that he
could see it.

I wondered if your museum might be interested in hosting my John Wayne
collection. I'd be happy to lend it to you at little or no cost, just because I'd like to
help celebrate the legacy of this great American. Perhaps we could call the
exhibit "Puttin' Up Our Dukes: A Tribute To John Wayne."

Thank you very much for your consideration.

Best Regards,

Sterling Huck
3901 Whitland Ave. #27
Nashville, TN 37205

Eden Park
Cincinnati, Ohio 45202-1596

Phone 513-721-5204
Fax 513-721-0129

CINCINNATI ART
M   U   S   E   U   M

August 28, 1996

Mr. Sterling Huck
3901 Whitland Ave. #27
Nashville, TN   37205

Dear Mr. Huck:

Thank you for your letter of August 26th and the generous offer to use your private collection of John Wayne related material. Unfortunately, our exhibition calendar is booked through the year 1999. However, I will forward your exhibition concept to the appropriate curator for future reference.

Thank you again for your interest and please feel free to provide us with any other suggestions. We are always looking for good exhibition ideas.

Sincerely,

Kathryn M. Haigh
Exhibitions and Registration Clerk

URGENT!!!!

July 17, 1998

Cracker Barrel Old Country Store
P.O. Box 787
Lebanon, TN 37088

Dear Cracker Barrel,

This is the second time I've written. I just want to confirm that beginning August 1st, 1998, I will be performing my one-man show, called Triple Bypass, at 28 Cracker Barrels through Tennessee and Alabama.

The show's title has two meanings. I grew up in Triple Bypass, Texas, and three years ago, I had triple bypass heart surgery. In my show, I weave funny and heartwarming stories about the south in with more serious warnings concerning cholesterol and the fat that clogs up arteries. I pick a banjo, stomp my feet, twirl my straw hat and smoke a corncob pipe (it's a prop, not real tobacco). I sing old favorites like Jerry Reed's "She Got The Gold, I Got The Shaft" in a medley with Isaac Hayes' "Shaft," and everyone claps along. This show will last approximately 2 hours and 40 minutes, with a brief intermission, during which maybe I can get a little of whatever the special is that day. Since my surgery, I have to be careful about eating too much fried okra or peach cobbler.

I'm rehearsing Triple Bypass now and I'm looking forward to bringing it to Cracker Barrel this summer. I have my own microphone. Please tell your booking agent, Mr. Jerry DePoot, that I'm grateful for this engagement and we can talk about the fee later.

Look out for Triple Bypass starring Sterling Huck, coming soon to Cracker Barrel!

Kind Regards,

Sterling Huck
3901 Whitland Ave. #27
Nashville, TN 37205

**Though not traditionally a venue
for big name entertainment,
Cracker Barrel did express an interest
in booking "Triple Bypass."**

**Unfortunately, they were
outbid by Stuckey's.**

Old Country Store
Box 787 • HARTMANN DRIVE
ON, TENNESSEE 37088-0787

Sterling Huck
3901 Whitland Avenue #27
Nashville, TN 37205

11530/4523

April 18, 2002

Columbus Zoo
9990 Riverside Dr.
Powell, OH 43065

Dear Columbus Zoo,

I am the manager of the hard rock group called Pachyderm! The band is currently putting the finishing touches on their debut record, to be released July 25th on Jumbo Records. The title is *Park Avenue Pachyderm*. We're still searching for the perfect CD cover shot. The concept we have in mind is to have the band members in fancy evening clothes, frolicking with some real live elephants, also in evening clothes (Jill, our talented seamstress, could fit the elephants for jackets and slacks if you give us their measurements). Maybe one of the elephants could wear a monocle and a top hat, set at a rakish angle. The band will be feeding caviar and champagne to these well-dressed pachyderms, and it will look like a posh uptown party.

If you have any available elephants for this photo shoot, we'd be very grateful. Of course, the Columbus Zoo will get full props in the liner notes of the record.

Thank you for your consideration. I look forward to hearing from you.

Kindest Regards,

Sterling Huck

Sterling Huck
3901 Whitland Ave. #27
Nashville, TN 37205

P.S. - Do elephants like rock music?

Columbus ZOO
and Aquarium
WWW.COLUMBUSZOO.ORG

April 23, 2002

Sterling Huck
3901 Whitland Ave. #27
Nashville, TN 37205

Dear Sterling:

Thank you for thinking of us. However, none of the elephants at the
Columbus Zoo are handleable and would not tolerate people standing near
them -- much less dressing them!

Good luck with your debut.

Patricia Peters
Associate Zoo Director/Marketing
Columbus Zoo and Aquarium

September 21, 1995

Gettysburg Travel Council
35 Carlisle St.
Gettysburg, PA 17325

Dear Gettysburg,

I'm an independent film maker, best known for *I'd Rather Be Reich*, the claymation version of the classic movie *Judgment At Nuremburg*.

Currently I'm working on an ambitious sci-fi/history picture, entitled *Ulysses S. Grant Meets The Saucer Men!* The basic premise for the movie is what I like to call a "What if . . .?" In this case, what if the Rebel forces had the help of aliens from outer space during the Civil War? How would the outcome have been affected??

The style of the film is campy, colorful and fun, with plenty of special effects and a soundtrack by the beloved Hawaiian entertainer Don Ho. The leading actor, who you may have heard of, is Indigo Matahi (*Heart Of Scrimshaw, A Dandy In Aspic*). We also have a tentative commitment for a cameo from Roy Clark.

I'm writing to request permission to film some key battle scenes at your Gettysburg site. I have a cast of approximately twenty-five, a crew of six, a chimp mascot named "Mumbles," and some large props, including a 20-ft. metallic saucer.

Thank you so much for your consideration of this proposal. I eagerly await your response.

Kind Regards,

Sterling Huck
3901 Whitland Ave. #27
Nashville, TN 37205

GETTYSBURG NATIONAL MILITARY PARK
EISENHOWER NATIONAL HISTORIC SITE
97 Taneytown Road
Gettysburg, Pennsylvania 17325

9/29/95

L30

Mr. Shuck
Re: U.S. Grant Meets the Saucer Men

Dear Film Permit Applicant:

Gettysburg National Military Park and Eisenhower National Historic Site require that any commercial filming or photography within the park by covered by a permit. The permit provides a means to keep activities in accordance with applicable regulations. Our goal is to both prevent any damage to the park resources and allow visitors to enjoy and learn from the park, while allowing appropriate filming to take place.

Please complete the enclosed application in black ink or with typewriter and submit it to this office by mail or during normal business hours Monday through Friday. Answer all questions, using "no" or "none" as appropriate, and include as much information as you can. Attach continuation sheets as needed. Return the completed application to: Superintendent, Gettysburg National Military Park, 97 Taneytown Road, Gettysburg, Pennsylvania, 17325. Applications for a special park use not received by this office 30 days prior to the event may not be considered.

After the event you may be billed for a $50.00 administrative fee and monitoring costs. This covers the expense of processing the permit from its inception through review and approval, routine monitoring, clean-up and final bookkeeping. Unbudgeted costs will also be billed if additional time and materials are expended by the park to manage the event. Depending upon the event, other requirements may include liability insurance and a performance bond. A Bill of Collection will be issued following your event for any monitoring costs.

If you have any questions, please feel free to contact me at (717) 334-1124.

Sincerely,

Laurie E. Coughlan
Management Assistant

Enclosure

PS: General Grant was not at or near the Battle of Gettysburg. He was fighting in the West. Try Vicksburg.

March 31, 2000

Dunkin' Donuts
8501 W. Higgins
Ste. 100
Chicago, IL 60631

Dear Dunkin' Donuts,

As a man who aspires to write and speak the King's English, I am appalled by the current state of grammar in our country. There are more contractions than in an overcrowded maternity ward and so many "g's" being dropped you would think we were all living in a Lil' Abner cartoon. But there should be no jubilation over this cornpone.

Your fine company can make a difference. As one of the most visible nationwide examples of the dropped "g," I urge you to restore the fallen letter to its rightful place. From now on, you can provide not only the best donuts and coffee, but a grammatical beacon to citizens everywhere by changing your name to Dunking Donuts.

I realize you have already established a precedent with the "n'(apostrophe)", but I think your store signs can be amended quite easily, without too much expense. In fact, I am willing to donate 1,000 orange "g's," hand cut from sturdy construction paper (I have not been able to shimmy up the pole to get to the sign at your Nashville location, so you will have to let me know about the exact dimensions of the letters).

Thanks for listening (not listenin') to me. Dunking Donuts - It sounds better, does it not? You even get a subliminal "king" in there to reinforce your supremacy over Krispy Kreme and Mister Donut.

I look forward to hearing from you, Dunking Donuts.

Best Regards,

Sterling Huck
3901 Whitland Ave. #27
Nashville, TN 37205

Dunkin' Donuts is doin' just fine, Sterlin'.

October 15, 2001

F & W Publications
1507 Dana Ave.
Cincinnati, OH 45207

Dear F & W,

I'm an author, best known for my novel *Playing Santiago*. It's a retelling of
Hemingway's classic *Old Man And The Sea*, from the marlin's point of view. I
was also co-writer on *Star Search Losers*, a pictorial survey of those who Ed
McMahon didn't pick on his talent show.

I'd like to pitch you my new work-in-progress, called *Robbing The Cradle:
How To Date A Woman Young Enough To Be Your Daughter*.

I'm a 48-year old bachelor who has a certain je ne sais quois with les jeunes
femmes. I've been seen out at popular nightclubs and other
establishments with beautiful young women on my arms. I can always hear
what other guys are thinking. They're thinking, "That lucky so-and-so. What's
he got that I haven't?"

My book distills all my know-how into a potent answer to that question.
Subjects covered include:

- How to "talk young"
- The psyche of 18-24 year olds
- Mathematical games to confuse her on the subject of age difference
- The fine line between suave and spooky
- The story of the old sea captain and the mermaid
- 21 surefire ways to avoid meeting her parents
- Sincerity vs. insincerity, and why both are your friends

If you please, I will gladly send you a chapter, or a finished manuscript of
*Robbing The Cradle: How To Date A Woman Young Enough To Be Your
Daughter*.

Thanks for your consideration.

Kind Regards,

Sterling Huck
3901 Whitland Ave. #27
Nashville, TN 37205

Writer's Digest Books • North Light Books • Betterway Books
Story Press • Popular Woodworking Books
Walking Stick Press • HOW Design Books

F&W Publications, Inc.
1507 Dana Avenue
Cincinnati, Ohio 45207
Phone 513 531-2690
FAX 513 531-7107

November 5, 2001

Sterling Huck
3901 Whitland Ave., #27
Nashville, TN 37205

Dear Mr. Huck:

Thank you for letting us consider publishing "Robbing the Cradle: How to Date a Woman Young Enough to be Your Daughter." Your topic is certainly interesting, but we don't feel that it's for us. Many excellent ideas just don't fit the range of books we feel would do well with the readers that we know we reach.

I hope you'll soon find an interested publisher. And thanks for thinking of Writer's Digest Books.

Sincerely,

Marylyn Alexander
Administrative Assistant
Writer's Digest Books

November 7, 2001

Hotel Norge
Ole Bulls Plass 4
N-5001 Bergen
Norway

Dear Hotel Norge,

I will be coming to Norway to perform at the Bergen Jazz Festival the week of February 15, 2002. If possible, I would like to stay at the beautiful Hotel Norge, about which I have heard so much.

My professional name is "Mr. Bumblebee." In my musical act, I play Rimsky-Korsakov's "Flight Of The Bumblebee" on twenty-two different instruments - from the fife to the tuba, from the bagpipes to the glockenspiel. *The Kansas City Sentinel* called me "magnificently precise and insistent . . . a stinger of an entertainer." *The New York Daily News* said, "Like being inside an angry hive . . ."

I'll be traveling with all my instruments and will be practicing "The Flight Of The Bumblebee" in the days leading up to my performance at the Jazz Festival. I don't think the music will bother your other guests - though the sousaphone has been known to rattle a few picture frames - but I thought I'd write ahead to get your permission. It's "The Flight Of The Bumblebee" on twenty-two different instruments, by "Mr. Bumblebee."

Thank you for your kind consideration. I look forward to hearing from you.

Best Regards,

Sterling Huck
3901 Whitland Ave. #27
Nashville, TN 37205
USA

Radisson SAS Hotel Norge
SAS Hotel Norge AS
Nedre Ole Bulls Plass 4
P.O. Box 662 Sentrum
N-5807 Bergen, Norway
Telephone: +47 55 57 30 00
Telefax: +47 55 57 30 01
www.radissonsas.com

3901 Whitlaand Ave nr. 27
Nashville, TN 37205
USA

Sterling Huck

Bergen, 22. November 2001

Dear Mr. Bumblebee

We were happy to receive you nice letter.

We do have available rooms in the requested period. We can offer you a price on Nok 995,- for a single room and 1195,- for a double room. If you want to upgrade your room to business class, that costs Nok 200,- more. We do not have any soundproof rooms for you, but could try to place you at a location that will not disturb the guests. We suppose you want to do some rehearsing.

Do you want any more information please do not hesitate to contact us again.

Looking forward to your visit.

Yours sincerely,

Katharina Hanson

Katharina Hanson

Katharina Hanson / Hotel Sales
Tlf. +47 55 57 30 23 - Fax: +47 55 57 30 31

Radisson SAS
HOTELS & RESORTS

Toll Free Reservations Norway: 800 160 91

Radisson SAS

CHUBBY ROBOT
PRECISE, EFFICIENT ROCK MUSIC

NO REPLY

October 21, 2001

Reynolds Wrap
6601 West Broad St.
Richmond, VA 23230

Dear Reynolds,

I play in a band called Chubby Robot (we used to be called Robotica but we had to change the name when we found out there was another group in Denmark with the same name). There are four of us in Chubby Robot, and as the name suggests, we are all chubby and we all dress as metallic men of rock music.

In our concert performances, we are completely sheathed in Reynolds Wrap aluminum foil, the shiny side out. When the lights hit us, it's a spectacular "Reynolds-tastic" reflection!! Your aluminum foil has made us one of the mid-South's hottest and shiniest live acts. At the end of the show, we wad up our costumes and throw the balls of foil out to the screaming fans. Some of our songs include "Chubby Robot Dance," "Foiled By Love," "Used To Be Tin," "Locked In Freshness Blues" and "Leftovers Again?"

We're now planning a winter tour (February-March 2002), and we'd like to ask if you might supply us with Reynolds Wrap for our costumes (we'd need approximately 25,000 feet). In exchange, Chubby Robot will plug your product during every show in every city.

I look forward to a collaboration between Reynolds Wrap and Chubby Robot!

Regards,

Sterling Huck

Sterling Huck
Chubby Robot
3901 Whitland Ave. #27
Nashville, TN 37205

P.S. - Our drummer Spudso is addicted to tongue twisters, and wanted me to have you try this one five times fast - "minimum aluminum."

April 14, 2002

Chef Boyardee
c/o ConAgra Foods, Inc.
Attn: Consumer Affairs
One ConAgra Drive
Omaha, NE 68102-5001

NO REPLY

Dear ConAgra,

I'm a composer/librettist whose musical shows have been staged around the country. My last creation, *Harland!* - based on the stormy life of fried chicken magnate Colonel Harland Sanders - won two Leonard M. Bankman Awards, one for Best Supporting actor (Indigo Matahi) and the other for Best Song ("Which Half Of The Wishbone?").

Currently, I'm developing my next project, tentatively entitled *Boyardee!* It's based on the life of the canned pasta maven, Hector Boiardi. My research has been hampered by a lack of good source material, so I was hoping you could answer a few questions for me about the man:

1. What was his political affiliation?

2. Is it true that the idea of miniature meatballs came to Boiardi after spending a weekend at the summer house of surrealist Salvador Dali?

3. When did the relationship between Boiardi and actress Brigitte Bardot begin and end?

4. Is there film footage available of Boiardi actually cooking his own recipes?

5. Was he comfortable with the phonetic spelling of his name printed on the chef's hat?

6. Is it true that he also invented the shoehorn?

Any assistance you could offer would be appreciated, as I'm scheduled to do a workshop staging of the piece with the Pulaski Players here in Tennessee this July. Thank you.

Kind Regards,

Sterling Huck
3901 Whitland Ave. #27
Nashville, TN 37205

November 21, 2001

The Thomas Tool Company.
85 East Badger Rd.
Racine, WI 53401

Dear Thomas Tools,

I am the president and founder of "Gay Blades," the nation's only touring musical saw group. There are eight young men, including myself, in the group. Each of us is an experienced "saw-ist," dedicated to preserving this endangered musical art.

Our repertoire includes everything from light classical to Broadway show tunes to soft-rock favorites such as "Winchester Cathedral," "Have You Never Been Mellow" and "I Will Always Love You." Currently we are preparing a special program, a birthday tribute to John Philip Sousa, called "Saws & Stripes Forever: Cutting Edge American Music," which we will be touring through ten Southern states this summer.

As you're no doubt aware, performing music on a saw is an exciting art and for the best pitch and timbre, requires a well-built tool. We have found that Thomas makes the best-sounding saws! Since the Gay Blades have had some financial difficulties of late (our last tour, a misjudged attempt to connect with a younger audience, called "Nine Inch Nails & A Really Sharp Saw," cost us plenty), we'd like to appeal to your company to underwrite a small part of our upcoming tour costs. In exchange for providing us with saws, we will heartily promote your line of fine tools.

Thank you for your consideration. I look forward to hearing from you.

Best Regards,

Sterling Huck
3901 Whitland Ave. #27
Nashville, TN 37205

T h o m a s   T o o l s
I n c o r p o r a t e d

_____85 East Badger Rd., Racine, WI 53401 (414-992-1700)_____

December 11, 2001

Sterling Huck
3901 Whiteland Ave. #27
Nashville, TN 37205

Dear Sterling:

Thank you for your letter of November 21, 2001. We're glad that your musical group has found a new use for our products.

Throughout the year, we receive frequent requests for donations and product samples from a variety of community service organizations. We do wish we had the capability to assist each and every one. Unfortunately, due to the volume of requests, we are unable to consider participation.

We regret that we are unable to assist your musical group, but wish you all success in your endeavors.

Sincerely,

Mickey Lyons
Consumer Represenative,
Thomas Tools Incorporated

cc:

July 12, 2001

Bluewind Restaurant & Club
In The Factory
230 Franklin Rd.
Franklin, TN 37221

Dear Bluewind,

This is to confirm my engagement on Saturday, August 18, 2001, at your establishment, performing my one-man show called Tanktop Scuzzball.

Assuming the role of an ornery, undereducated ferris wheel operator named Bobby Joe Neal, I entertain the audience for two hours (one 15-minute intermission) with rants, stories, songs and physical threats. I wear a mesh tank top and a chest pelt.

Bobby Joe is a colorful character who believes in America, carnivals, good hooch, and getting his fair share of both paychecks and pork rinds. The Lewisburg Gazette (Lewisburg, AK) called me "Don Rickles from the holler!" and The Blue Ash Monitor (Blue Ash, OH) said, "Tanktop is a red, white and VERY blue look at America the not so beautiful!"

I'm looking forward to performing Tanktop Scuzzball at Bluewind next month.

Regards,

Sterling Huck
3901 Whitland Ave. #27
Nashville, TN 37205

P.S. - I like to get my money up front.

BLUEWIND JAZZ CLUB
LOCATED INSIDE THE FACTORY AT FRANKLIN
230 FRANKLIN ROAD 11-Y
FRANKLIN, TN   37065
615-599-4995

July 18, 2001

Sterling Huck
3901 Whitland Ave. #27
Nashville, TN 37205

Sterling Huck:

I have received your letter of July 12, 2001. I'm sorry but we have no record of your booking a performance of "Tanktop Scuzzball" at Bluewind on Saturday, Aug 18th. Please adjust your schedule accordingly.

If you have further questions, please call us at 615-599-4995.

Sincerely,

Joel Arnold
Manager of Bluewind

August 1, 1996

Victoria's Secret
P.O. Box 16590
Columbus, OH 43216

Dear Victoria's Secret,

As an aspiring professional shutterbug, I've long admired the layouts and pictures of shapely women modeling lingerie in your catalogs. Your photographer certainly has an eye for beauty and for that "right moment" when to click.

I don't know how you go about hiring photographers but I'd like to make a bold offer of my services, which could be provided at a low cost with guaranteed results. My professional experience is varied: an office supply catalog, a power tool brochure and most recently, the *Clown Yearbook*.

I'm including a few samples for your inspection. While it may seem a leap from photographing a belt sander and Mr. Buttons to capturing a lovely lingerie model on film, I feel confident that I could deliver the goods for your company.

Please let me know what the next step is. I'm looking forward to a long association with Victoria's Secret.

Best Regards,

Sterling Huck
3901 Whitland Ave. #27
Nashville, TN 37205

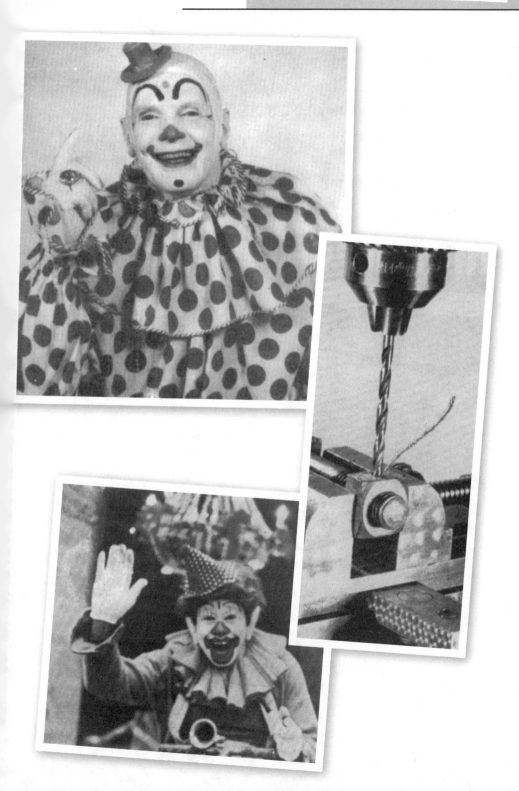

Given his current portfolio,
Victoria's Secret did not feel that
Sterling was quite ready for a career
in high fashion photography.

October 25, 2001

Sterling Huck
The "Looky, looky" guy

Register Of Copyrights
The Library Of Congress
Washington, DC 20557

Dear Copyright Office,

From Oliver Hardy twiddling his tie to Jack Benny slapping a hand to his cheek, from Jimmy Walker yelling "Dy-No-Mite!" to Gallagher smashing a watermelon with a sledgehammer, America's funniest comedians have always had a signature gesture or line that makes them instantly recognizable.

As a young, aspiring funny man, I have developed my own gesture and line. I move my left hand in a fast circular motion, as if I'm wiping a dirty window, then say, "Looky, looky!" This is a tagline I attach to a lot of my humorous anecdotes and jokes. The audiences have become so fond of my gesture and tagline that they often shout it along with me.

I would like to copyright my circular hand motion (I do it 6 1/2 times) plus "Looky, looky!" as an insurance policy against other comedians stealing this crucial part of my act. Should I send a videotape of me onstage?

Time is of the essence. My star is on the rise and I need to protect my precious creative material.

Looky, looky,

Sterling Huck
3901 Whitland Ave. #27
Nashville, TN 37205

February 23, 2002

Phoenixville Railroad Museum
P.O. Box 610520
Philadelphia, PA 19560

Dear Phoenixville Railroad Museum,

For nearly forty years, I've been collecting bindlestiffs. Many of these precious American artifacts date back to the turn of the 20th century. Though the hobos and tramps who carried them have been forgotten, the bindlestiffs live on. And I have them.

My collection, which is close to 170 bindlestiffs, has outgrown my modest dwelling, and so I would like to humbly offer to donate them for permanent exhibition to your museum. I think it would be a highly emotional experience for your visitors to see an endless row of bindlestiffs. Kind of like the Vietnam Veterans memorial, but for hobos.

Many of the soiled red bandanas have never been untied from their sticks, so I don't know what their contents are. Harmonicas? Oats? Old bent spoons? Money? Tins of wax? That's the mystery of the bindlestiff, and why I've been collecting them most of my life.

I've talked to a few couriers, including Federal Express, about a special "bindlestiff" rate, so I'm sure I could send you a few hundred of my most treasured pieces for a good price.

Thank you for considering this offer. I look forward to your response.

Best Regards,

Sterling Huck
3901 Whitland Ave. #27
Nashville, TN 37205

P.S. - I have a "stage prop" bindlestiff that belonged to the clown Emmett Kelly, Jr.

PHOENIXVILLE RAILROAD MUSEUM

PHOENIXVILLE RAILROAD MUSEUM, P.O. BOX 601520, PHOENIXVILLE, PA 19560

March 2, 2002

Sterling Huck
3901 Whitland Ave. #27
Nashville, TN 37205

Dear Sterling:

Thank you for your letter and your kind offer of your bindlestiff collection.

Currently, we do not have display areas for showcasing railroad artifacts and related items. If we accepted your collection as a donation, we would have to store it until such time as we are able to display the many artifacts we too have collected.

I would guess you'll be offering the collection to other railroad museums around the country as well. If you haven't already, you might try approaching the Florida Gulf Coast Railroad Museum or the New York Central Railroad Museum.

I can only imagine how interesting your collection is. I wouldn't have had the willpower to not peek into some of those bandanas!

Sincerely Yours,

Glenn O' Malley
Phoenixville Railroad Museum

NO REPLY

April 16, 2002

Stadsbestuur Oostende
Vindictivelaan 1
8400 Oostende, Belgium

Dear Friends in Oostende,

I am a choreographer and the recipient of the 2001 Leonard M. Bankman Award for my cable television special, *Jazzercise With Wolves*. As the title suggests, the program combines expressive modern dance, Native American folk dancing and the training of highly dangerous wolves. *The Minneapolis Star Tribune* said, " . . . this is a wow of a pow-wow! Imagine Deni Terio meets Jack London." And the *Blue Ash Monitor* said, "Somewhere, Lon Chaney, Jr. is smiling."

I would like to perform this show live and in person in Oostende this summer.

I look forward to your swift response. Let's dance!

Fond Regards,

Sterling Huck
3901 Whitland Ave. #27
Nashville, TN 37205
USA

P.S. - Are there really mermaids in Oostende?

Pet Sniper
(Black Veil Records)

March 17, 1998

Girl Scouts Of America
420 Fifth Avenue
14th Floor
New York, NY 10018-2798

Greetings GSA,

I am the manager of a heavy metal rock band called Pet Sniper. They've sold over one million copies worldwide (they're huge in the Scandanavian countries) of their first four albums, *Infrared, The Velocity Of Love, Mantenna* and *Doctor Rockingstone, I Presume*.

Currently the guys are in the studio, putting the finishing touches on their latest album, which will be released August 14, 1998 on Black Veil Records.

For the cover art, they'd like to photograph themselves, posing with their instruments, amidst a large crowd of Girl Scouts. The tentative title of the album is *Get 'Em While They're Young*. I realize you may think this is in questionable taste, but let me assure you that the members of Pet Sniper are hardworking family-oriented gentlemen. Thumper, the drummer, has two lovely daughters, 5 and 7, and El-Moz, the lead guitarist, is the proud papa of an 18 month old baby boy. The picture would have a spirit of fun and light-heartedness to it, and I'm sure the girls would enjoy meeting Pet Sniper. We could even arrange for complimentary band T-shirts and posters for the Girl Scouts!

We'd like to arrange the shoot to coincide with one of your large regional or national conventions, so we can get the maximum amount of Girl Scouts. Could you please suggest a time and place (and also advise me of the fee) so we could set up this photo shoot? It needs to be done by July 1st at the latest.

Thank you so much for working with my band Pet Sniper. I look forward to your reply

Regards,

Sterling Huck
3901 Whitland Ave. #27
Nashville, TN 37205

December 19, 1995

Winchester Cathedral
Winchester Hants SO23 9LS
England

Dear Sirs,

I'm an independent director scouting locations for my new science fiction movie entitled *Zarbu, The Mutant From Beyond*. Recently, at a dinner party in New Orleans, I bumped into one of your custodians, Mr. Trevor Shilley. He suggested I write.

One of my film's key scenes - where the space monster Zarbu (currently being built by effects wizard Indigo Matahi) defends its larvae from military forces - is to take place inside an old cathedral.

As an artist who appreciates classic architecture of the religious kind, I immediately thought of your cathedral and how much it would add to the drama and atmosphere of the scene. And if the movie is successful at the box office, it might be good publicity for both of us, if you catch my drift.

So, would it be possible to perhaps have the use of the cathedral's interior for 18-24 hours? My actors and crew are very flexible, and since we have a healthy budget, travel arrangements are no problem. Of course, we'd respect the grounds and structure at Winchester and would clean up afterwards (Zarbu does secrete a sticky substance, but it's non-corrosive and easily removed with paint thinner).

Thanks for your consideration of this proposal, and please say hello to Mr. Shilley for me.

Best Regards,

Sterling Huck
3901 Whitland Ave. #27
Nashville, TN 37205
USA

WINCHESTER CATHEDRAL

The Dean and Chapter of Winchester

The Cathedral Office, 5 The Close, Winchester, Hampshire SO23 9LS

Telephone: (01962) 853137   Facsimile: (01962) 841519

From the Receiver General
Keith Bamber

8 January 1996

Mr Sterling Huck
3901 Whitland Avenue #27
Nashville
TN 37205
U S A

Dear Mr Huck

<u>Zarbu, The Mutant From Beyond</u>

Thank you for your letter dated 19 December.

I am sorry that we cannot close the Cathedral for filming for 18-24 hours as you suggest as services are held here each day and we must be open to congregations as well as visitors.   It might have been fun watching Zarbu defending its larvae from military forces. However, we could not have allowed any sticky substance to be secreted on any part of the building, and even less, the paint thinner to remove it.

I think you will find this response typical of custodians of medieval buildings who may well assume that it would be more simple and less expensive to build sets for what you require nearer your home base.

Yours sincerely

Keith Bamber.

November 10, 2001

Government of India
Tourist Office
B.K. Kakati Rd.
Uluberi, Guwahati 781-007
India

Dear India,

I have a one-man show that I would like to bring to your country. It's called "Hindi Hit Parade!" Over the course of 90 minutes, I reinterpret classic American popular songs with a decidedly "Indian flavor."

I've included a sample lyric from my catalog of special material. It's called "The Curry With The Fringe On Top" (it's sung to the tune of Rodgers & Hammerstein's "The Surrey With The Fringe On Top"). Other numbers in my show include "Too Darn Mahatma," "The Thrill Is Gandhi" and "Whose Sari Now?"

I also do impressions of famous American singers with an Indian flavor - Judy Garlindjiv, Cal Cuttaway and Frank Sumatra. I'm working on Bing Crosbijajib.

I hope that you can offer help with the booking of my show into appropriate venues and nightclubs throughout your country (I don't mind sharing a bill). My asking price is usually $250 plus meals (do you have turkey burgers?). Also, I travel with a large tape recorder (tracks for my songs), so I'll need to know if the voltage in India is different from the U.S.

I am now looking forward to when I will sing the "Hindi Hit Parade" for all my friends in India, you know.

See you soon. Let me know what you think of the enclosed lyric.

Kindest Regards,

Sterling Huck
3901 Whitland Ave. #27
Nashville, TN 37205
USA

"The Curry With The Fringe On Top"
(sung to the tune of "The Surrey With The Fringe On Top")

If you're hungry for some Tandoori,
there's a place that serves in a hurry,
but careful you don't eat any curry
with the fringe on top.
Watch that fringe and see if it's fuzzy,
taste a bit and then if it's scuzzy,
ask the happy Hindi waiter does he
want to swap.
If the rice is green
and the gravy is blue,
the chicken tougher than leather.
If you're stomach starts hurtin'
and your head does too,
and you feel as light as a feather.
Make a beeline straight for the toilet,
you're on this date, you don't want to spoil it,
a brand new shirt, you can't bear to soil it,
but you just can't stop
throwing up the curry with the fringe on the top!

lyrics by Sterling Huck

February 25, 2002

Chamber Of Commerce
309 State St.
Weiser, ID 83672
Attn: Old-Time Fiddlers' Contest & Festival

Dear COC,

My name is Sterling Huck and I am the world's only naked old-time fiddler. I'd like to join your Old-Time Fiddlers' Contest & Festival this June.

A little background on me: I've been playing the fiddle since I was five years old. I am now sixty-eight. In my twenties, I discovered that I play much better if I shed every stitch of clothing. Now it's the only way I can play. I don't do anything lewd or untoward with the fiddle or bow. I just fiddle up a storm, and I happen to be naked while I'm doing it. If it's sunny I'll wear a cowboy hat. I actually own the one that Clark Gable wore in *The Misfits*. I've developed a lot of technique and can play "Turkey In The Straw" in quintuple time.

I've been fiddling at nudist resorts such as Whispering Pines and Banana Patch for years, but honestly, those people aren't much interested in fiddling. I want to be among my own kind.

I hope you'll extend an invitation to me for your festival in June.

Best Regards,

Sterling Huck

Sterling Huck
3901 Whitland Ave. #27
Nashville, TN 37205

National Oldtime
Fiddlers' Contest® and Festival

309 STATE STREET
WEISER, IDAHO 83672
PHONE (208) 414-0452
www.fiddlecontest.com

HISTORIC WEISER, IDAHO

THIRD FULL WEEK IN JUNE

April 23, 2002

Sterling Huck
3901 Whitland Ave #27
Nashville TX 37205

Sterling,

Thank you for your interest in the National Oldtime Fiddlers' Contest and Festival. We considered your request for an invitation to our contest to be held in June this year. We would be happy to welcome you to Weiser, but we could not condone the lack of appropriate clothing. We take great pride in offering a family event and do not feel nakedness would fit in well.

If you decide you would like to enter our contest and conform to our standards, please check out our website: www.fiddlecontest.com and register on-line or call this office and request a contestant packet.

Best regards,

Sue Amano

Sue Amano

1952 ～ 50 Years ～ 2002